2-6-75

WRITING FOR INDUSTRY

RAYMOND C. TRACY

Publications Engineer and Publications Manager
Instructor at Utah Technical College and at
University of Utah Institute of Technological Training

HAROLD L. JENNINGS

Specifications Supervisor and
Technical Services Supervisor

 American Technical Society * Chicago 60637

Preface

Clear and concise writing is essential in modern industry. Communications of all kinds must be prepared on the job: accident reports, inspection reports, project reports, specifications, bids, proposals, letters, etc. In addition, job applications must be filled out accurately and clearly.

The purpose of this text is to teach students the skills needed for effective industrial writing. This is done as directly and simply as possible, using examples found on the job in all phases of industry and the trades.

The exercises are designed to teach the student to organize his material logically without omitting any essential details. Good punctuation and grammar are taught while preparing reports and writing letters covering practical situations found in all occupational areas. Both written and spoken subjects are covered.

The Publishers

Contents

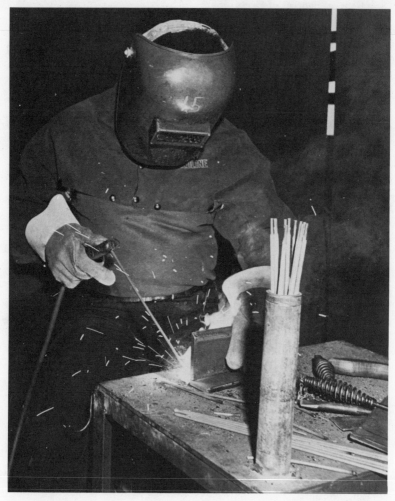

In a few seconds this welder will witness an accident. He will look up just in time to see a 4" × 4" wood stacking block fall from the load of an overhead crane. "Look out," he shouts to his fellow workman. But his warning is too late. The heavy block strikes his companion on his helmet and shoulder, knocking him to the ground. His collar bone is broken.

In an investigation of the accident, the welder is asked to write a detailed report of what he saw at the time of the accident. He is asked to write why the accident happened, and what could have been done to prevent such accidents. (Singer Safety Products, Inc.)

CHAPTER 1

The Need for Vocational Writing

The increasing importance of *written communications* in the technical, trade, and business fields is illustrated by the ever increasing demand for qualified vocational specialists who can also write. *Qualified* in this sense means that the vocational specialist not only knows his job and understands a specific job situation, but that he is also capable of accurately describing in writing what he sees and does.

If the information you write in a letter or report is incomplete or misunderstood, you could receive the wrong parts of equipment for a job and thus cause construction to be delayed. In seeking employment, if your application is not properly prepared you may not get the position you wish. If you should fail to accurately report the cause of an accident in a written report, it could leave others exposed to unseen danger. Therefore, the primary task in vocational communications is to take disorganized and unfamiliar material and to make it meaningful to other people through writing.

In many jobs today the most skillful and productive person may be severely handicapped if he or she is unable to write with an acceptable degree of accuracy and clarity. This applies to more jobs than we at first might think. Few people, for example, foresee the need to prepare an industrial accident report. Unfortunately, we are not always able to choose the one that will have to prepare such a report. Yet, the prevention of the same type accident in the future may depend upon the ability of someone to clearly and accurately report the details of what happened.

In preparing a report about an accident involving a forklift truck, the following description of what occurred would be almost useless:

> After a lot of trouble the fork-lift truck driver worked up to the stacks of crates, picked up a pallet of crates and backed up. He turned and started out the same way that he had gone in. When he was about halfway down the loading dock, he was going too fast and the wheel went off the edge of the dock. The truck tumbled to the ground. The driver jumped clear.

This might be adequate for a newspaper account of what happened. But for a safety manager charged with the responsibility of making sure this type of accident does not happen again, there are few facts in this description which he can use to draw conclusions and make recommendations.

The safety manager would find the following description of the same accident far more useful:

> The driver brought the fork-lift truck to the loading dock to pick up a pallet of crates filled with metal parts. The driver had difficulty positioning the truck because crates of other material blocked the entrance. When he was able to pick up the pallet of crates he backed the truck out very slowly and moved along the edge of the dock. This was the only route that he could use because crates were stacked everywhere on the dock except along the edge.
>
> As the truck moved along the dock it suddenly gained speed. The right front wheel hit the six-inch railing along the edge of the dock. Before the driver could react, the wheel had jumped over the railing and the truck fell to the ground which is four feet below the top of the railing. As the truck hit the ground and turned over on the right side, the driver jumped clear to avoid injury.

From the second description of the accident, the safety manager can find a number of steps that should be taken to prevent such an accident in the future. This description focused on the important details. If not correctly focused writing is often of no value to the reader.

What Is a Report?

A report, whether it be in the form of letter, a memorandum, or in text format, has one basic purpose: to tell all the necessary facts about a given situation, with few words, and in a manner that the reader will have no major questions left to ask.

Who Uses Reports?

We all do. When you write a personal letter to a friend, it is a simplified report form—explaining your activities, experiences, and feelings.

On the business level there are 2.5 to 3.0 million secretaries, stenographers, and typists in the United States. If each of these employees prepared only two letters per day, it represents between 5 and 6 million letters and approximately 1.8 billion words!

These letters cost about $60 million per day to prepare. So it is no wonder that industrial and business supervisors want good, concise, effective writing at minimum cost.

Thousands of memoranda and reports are also generated each day by various manufacturing and service industries, as well as business, technical, and scientific facilities throughout the nation. These documents usually require even greater effort and skill in preparation than a letter, thus the cost per page is significantly higher than the cost of business letter production.

The vocational specialist, whether he is employed by a company or is self-employed, should be trained to express himself moderately well in writing. He should know how to write such documents as job progress reports, business letters, work bid proposals, job applications and resumés, grievance reports, production progress reports, test reports, equipment evaluation reports, accident reports, etc. Chapter 10 presents examples of various report subjects, formats and styles.

Needed Skills for Writing Reports

The problems of expression in vocational and technical communications are basically the same as those found in conveying ideas in any other written work. The same care must be taken in sentence construction, paragraph construction, and overall organization. However, vocational writing is quite different from literary or creative writing in that it deals primarily with facts. These facts should be explained in clear, straightforward writing.

Telling things in the order in which they happened is important in vocational communications, and the writer should be careful to describe just what happened without showing personal attitudes or feelings. The facts must be arranged so clearly that the reader will be convinced by reason.

Example

Many companies give cash awards for useful suggestions made by employees who submit their suggestions in writing. Here are separate suggestions made by two employees who operate a manufacturing machine:

First employee:

> This *blankety* roller press keeps bustin' all the time. Let's get the *blankety-blank* thing fixed.

Second employee:

> Unfortunately, the No. 2 roller press has had seven mechanical failures in the past month. These failures have made department production drop by 20 percent.
>
> I believe the failures were caused by improper lubrication of the left lever bearings. I therefore suggest that inspections of those bearings be made more often by maintenance personnel and more lubricating performed as indicated by the inspections.

If you were a supervisor receiving these suggestions, which employee do you think should get paid for his suggestion?

The vocational writer explains material through the use of definitions, comparisons, and details. Therefore, it is important that he have a knowledge of the field in which he works. The untrained writer overlooks important details and fails to distinguish the essential from the irrelevant. But a modern vocational writer must not only be able to meet the standards of his industrial or business specialty, but he must also be able to meet the standards of good writing.

Good Report Writing

Effective writing consists of many seemingly complex elements which really aren't all that complicated. These elements include: vocabulary, spelling, grammar, punctuation, knowledge of subject, logic and word arrangement:

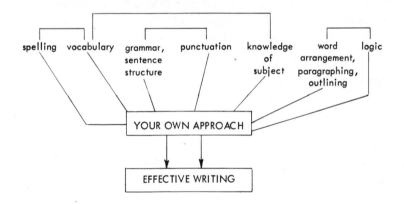

Your Vocabulary

English is a very rich language with more than 450,000 words in current use, as indicated by *Webster's New International Dictionary of the English Language.*

The person educated through high-school will possess a reading vocabulary of 15 to 20 thousand words. Fortunately, we all learn approximately the same words. Otherwise we could not communicate with one another. These words, which you have stored in your memory bank, are the basis of almost everything you do. You cannot think and reason without words and you can't solve problems without thinking in terms of words.

In communications, you effectively use two kinds of working vocabularies: a general knowledge of nontechnical words, and specific knowledge of technical words.

How do you know if you have a sufficient number of the right words in your vocabulary? Well, look at it this way: if you find many words in your reading that you do not understand, you know you need vocabulary study. When you come across an unfamiliar word, take the time to look it up in a dictionary.

There are many good vocabulary study books available in low-cost paperback form at magazine shops and bookstores. Most vocational and technical books have a glossary of terms in the back of the book. If you obtain a useful vocabulary list, and learn just three new words each day, in one year you will have added more than 1,000 new words to your vocabulary.

Using the Dictionary

A good desk size dictionary is recommended for solving vocational reading and writing reference problems, including:[1]

(1) Spelling
(2) Pronunciation
(3) Word meaning
(4) Determining parts of speech

Let's say, for example, that you hear one of your instructors use the word *symmetrical* in his classroom lecture. He said that duplex dwellings for housing two families are built in a symmetrical fashion.

---

[1]*Webster's New Collegiate Dictionary*, published by G & C Merriam Co. is an example. Others include the *Webster's College* edition, the *Random House Dictionary*, and the *American Heritage Dictionary*.

You write the word in your notes, but you are not sure of the proper spelling, pronunciation, meaning, or part of speech. What do you do? Look it up in your dictionary, of course!

You have spelled the word this wrong way: *simetricle.*

You look in your dictionary, but find there is no such word listed. Therefore, assume that your spelling is wrong. Well, what next? First, try to think how the word might be spelled in another way:

semetricle sametricle symetricle

Semetricle and *sametricle* cannot be found in the dictionary either. However, looking for symetricle, you find a very similar word: *symmetrical.* The meaning of this word fits the discussion in your notes, thus you are reasonably certain that you now have located the right word. And you have the proper spelling.

Proper pronunciation is indicated by the words shown between the marks.

sə-'me-tri-kəl

To determine the correct pronunciation, turn to the table on the inside front cover of your dictionary. For example:

s = the "s" sound in *s*ource
ə = the "a" sound in b*a*nana
m = the "m" sound in *m*urmer
e = the "e" sound in b*e*t
t = the "t" sound in *t*ie
r = the "r" sound in *r*are
i = the "i" sound in t*i*p
k = the "c" sound in *c*ook
l = "l" sound in *l*ily

By putting these individual sounds together, you can properly pronounce the word. Try it.

To determine the part of speech *symmetrical* may be, look for the indicator following the pronunciation example. It lists *adj,* meaning that symmetrical is always an adjective.

Most words have several meanings or variations of meanings. The dictionary lists these meanings in numerical order,
with the first meaning being the most common one in current
use. The first meaning is:

1. having, involving, or exhibiting symmetry;

So the dictionary has defined the word *symmetrical* by referring you to the word *symmetry*.

Looking down to the word symmetry, it means something
that has balanced proportions. A duplex dwelling for two
families is usually symmetrical, because it has the same
number and type of rooms on either side of the center of the
building.

Learning to use the dictionary is like any other skill. The
more you do it, the better you will become at being able to use
it well.

Spelling Re-examined

Unfortunately, there are few spelling rules which do not
have exceptions:

"i before e *except* after c, or when pronounced as ā in neigh-
bor or weigh. But what about such words as: weird, being,
deify, height, heifer, reiterate, seismograph, either, neither,
seize, leisure, and species? So the rules are only a partial help.

There are about 44 sounds in the English language with 26
letters and combinations of those letters used to write the
sounds. Generally, vowels (a, e, i, o, u and sometimes y) have
more than one sound:

a—(as in) : banana day

map   father

However, spelling by sound is not always effective as was
illustrated by the word symmetrical in the section above.
Furthermore, some words sound alike but are spelled differ-
ently, and mean different things:

aloud, allowed	flower, flour	stationery, stationary
bear, bare	fourth, forth	threw, through
blue, blew	foreword, forward	to, too, two
course, coarse	it's, its	whole, hole
dear, deer	hear, here	who's, whose
died, dyed	principle, principal	write, right, rite

At this stage of your education, you basically know when you write a word down whether you're sure of the proper spelling. So if you're not sure about the spelling, use a substitute word or look up the questionable word in the dictionary.

Actually, there are only about 500 common words that we frequently misspell. If you have difficulty in spelling, it is suggested that you obtain a paperback book on spelling and learn two or three new words each day—using brute force memory if no other method works for you. Here is a list of 75 commonly misspelled words. If you know how to spell these words, you are well on your way to solving the spelling problem.

WORD LIST

accessible	eighth	personnel
accommodate	exceed	plain
accurate	exhaust	plane
achieve	factory	precede
affect	forth	principal
allowed	fourth	principle
all right	freight	problem
almost	gage (or gauge)	procedure
alter	governor	proceed
altogether	hear	quantity
among	here	recede
amount	holiday	receive
analyze	hundred	safety
apparatus	length	seize
argument	license	sieve
bearing	maintenance	similar
bulletin	manual	specimen
category	material	stationary
changeable	mechanics	stationery
chosen	mileage	succeed
controlled	ninety	superintendent
description	ninth	technique
device	parallel	thorough
divide	perform	transferred
effect	permanent	vacuum

Understanding Basic Grammar

Grammar is the study of all those rules that treat the construction, form, and use of words. Without a useful knowledge of grammar, good writing is difficult to achieve.

Specifically, a knowledge of grammar is a working knowledge of the eight basic parts of speech and the associated gerunds, infinitives, participles, phrases, and clauses.

Table I presents a comparison of these elements.

Most people who write successfully do not necessarily think in terms of the basic parts of speech all the time, unless they have a specific problem to solve in a given sentence. But they learned to use these elements properly at one time in their educational careers and have kept proper habits.

A grammar review is presented for your use in Appendix A.

Punctuation Made Easy

Punctuation consists of 13 marks and symbols that are used in sentence construction to make the words more meaningful. Proper punctuation can mean the difference between effective writing and sentences which cannot be understood. These marks include the *period, comma, semicolon, colon, question mark, exclamation point, apostrophe, parenthesis, single quotation mark, double quotation mark, hyphen, dash,* and *ellipsis.*

Appendix B lists easy-to-follow punctuation rules for your reference and review.

Knowledge of Subject

A writer must know what he is talking about. He will fool no one by trying to fake it.

Professional writers are so aware of this requirement that some have gone to extreme lengths to gain new insight. For example, one sports writer played as a quarterback in an exhibition game between two professional teams; another writer put on the gloves, fought, and was knocked out by a heavyweight, world's champion prize fighter.

TABLE I. ELEMENTS OF A SENTENCE

Element	Function in Sentence
noun pronoun gerund infinitive gerund phrase infinitive phrase noun clause	can be a subject, direct object, indirect object, subjective complement or objective complement
verbs auxilliary verbs	words which express action, existence, or occurrence
adjective possessive pronoun participle infinitive prepositional phrase infinitive phrase adjective clause	modifies a noun, pronoun, or another element being used as a noun
adverb prepositional phrase infinitive infinitive phrase adverbial clause	may modify a verb, an adjective, another adverb, or another element being used as an adjective or adverb
preposition	introduces prepositional phrase
conjunction	connective word
interjection	words used in place of a sentence to express strong feeling or emotion

Applied Logic

When we say something isn't logical, what do we really mean? We mean that a conclusion is not proven to be correct. **Fact Analysis.** Some statements are simply wrong in fact:

> "Use of a 16-penny gun to drive nails in house framing is an excellent example of the use of hydraulic air compression principles."

The author of the above sentence simply doesn't know what he is talking about. There is no such thing as a *"hydraulic air compression principle"!* It's nonsense!

Argument Analysis. Logic in the formal sense involves the use of an argument which consists of a *major premise,* a *minor premise,* and a *conclusion:*

> *Major Premise:* All copper wire will conduct electric current.
> *Minor Premise:* This rod is copper wire.
> _____
> *Therefore:* This rod will conduct electric current.

The above argument seems sound enough. But what if one of the premises were false? What if the rod were really made from plastic? The conclusion would also be false. The individual writing the argument either lied or was fooled by the appearance of the rod and did not test it properly to determine its composition.

Another kind of fuzzy thinking involves drawing a false conclusion that is based on sound *premises:*

> All copper wire will conduct electric current.
> Electric current will flow through this wire.
> _____
> Therefore: This wire is copper wire.

The fault here, of course, is that many metals can be made into wire and will conduct electricity. The writer didn't consider all the alternatives.

Many vocational writers have these poor reasoning processes in their reports. Each of us should try to guard against such false statements which most often occur when attempting to write long, involved sentences.

Word Arrangement

Example No. 1

A meeting to determine what technical information is needed in the company's annual report on recent company production improvements will be held. It'll be on Monday. Meet at three p.m.; and bring all necessary support to discuss them with personnel who will be in attendance and will be responsible for making up the report after the meeting is completed at 4:30 p.m.

Example No. 2

You are requested to attend a meeting on Monday, April 19, from 3-4:30 p.m., in the Administration Building conference room. Recent company production improvements will be discussed, and technical information on these improvements will be summarized for inclusion in the company's annual report. Please be prepared to discuss your role in developing these improvements, and bring appropriate data to support your discussion.

Notice that the thoughts expressed in the first example have poor arrangement; the paragraph does not even say where the meeting will be held; it does not tell the reader what kind of support to bring. The second example paragraph has much better word arrangement. First it *asks* the recipient to attend the scheduled meeting and then answers all reasonable questions.

Your Own Approach

In vocational communications, writing cannot always be accomplished according to a formula. Sometimes you will need to use your own original approach. When highly involved writing is required, because of a complex subject or situation, five mental stages are ordinarily observed as the writer struggles to solve his problem:

Preparation. The writer must have all the necessary information and facts at hand. (See Chapter 6, "Gathering Facts and Sorting Data"; and Chapter 7, "Planning the Report.")

Resting Stage. After reviewing and studying the situation, the writer deliberately stops thinking about the matter for a while. During this period, some of the complex thoughts which were interfering with simple organization will tend to fade away. He should make an outline before starting to present his facts. (See Chapter 4, "The Approach" and Chapter 7, "Planning the Report.") Organization becomes important here in making certain that your approach will be understood by others.

Idea Stage. The writer gets a good idea and tests it by starting to write. If the idea has no hitches, he will complete the *first* rough draft by following his outline.

Evaluation. Usually, so-called *good ideas* are incomplete, and necessary details are lacking. The writer studies his rough draft and determines its inadequacies.

Reconstruction. The writer must then reconstruct, rewrite, and edit his rough draft. (See Chapter 11, "Editing and Proofreading.")

In examining the above approach, it is obvious that some mental activity comes before the actual writing begins.

Let's again examine the two sample paragraphs discussed previously in this chapter under *Word Arrangement*. The improved second paragraph is not what we would call high quality writing, but it is easier to read, more necessary facts are presented, and the writing has a more logical organization. Thus it may be said to be more effective than the first example.

EXERCISES

1. In two or three sentences tell what a report is.

2. Estimate what it would cost to write a two-page business letter, have it typed by a secretary, proofread it, correct it, and have it mailed.

3. Define 25 of the following terms, using your dictionary and any other reference sources. Your instructor will assist you with those terms you are unable to define on your own.

General terms:

clockwise	picket	vertical
counterclockwise	profit	portable
license	supervision	flexibility
correspondence	foreman	modular
memorandum	management	conventional
symmetrical	brotherhood	diagonal
vocation	technology	blueprint
journeyman	mechanism	diagram
vowel	apprentice	inspector
consonant	trade	structure
contract	guarantee	partial
collective bargaining	invoice	fabrication
obsolete	overtime	rectangular
strike	grievance	elevation
walk out	plan	beveled
	horizontal	

4. All of the following words (except two) are misspelled. Can you spell them correctly?

acheive	fourty	recieve
alright	holaday	repetishon
catagory	lisence	seperate
definately	maintainence	simalar
dissappear	mispelling	suceed
dissapoint	ninty	supertindant
dissatisfaction	preceede	truley
existance	procede	vacum

5. Read the following paragraph:

> When connecting his portable saw to the 110 volt electrical power source, Mr. Davis used an extension cord that was not equipped with a ground wire. I noticed the condition and called his attention to it. He laughed and said he had used that cord for years and nothing had ever happened yet. But it had been raining the night before and, to be safe, I again asked him to change the cord. Nothing was done, however, and sawing began.

Write *one* example beside each part of speech below, taking your example from the above paragraph:

- a. Independent clause
- b. Prepositional phrase (acting as an adverb)
- c. Participle
- d. Gerund
- e. Auxiliary verb
- f. Dependent clause (acting as adjective)
- g. Four different pronouns
- h. Proper noun
- i. Infinitive
- j. Conjunction
- k. Pronoun acting as an adjective

6. Read the following paragraph and correct any punctuation errors:

> When Mr. Evans made his offer to buy this tool equipment he neglected to state a bid price his bid is therefore not allowed. Subsequently 50000 items from Allen-Jones Steel Company tool stock were sold to another buyer for a savings, after taxes of $5000.00.

7. What is logically wrong with this argument?

> Our oscilloscopes have a wide variety of optional attachments, including a Polaroid camera setup for photographing scope patterns. Buy our Model 1370 today and save.

8. Try to rewrite the following memorandum, correcting all the errors you see.

On the morning of July 17, we will hold a meeting to discuss tardyness by manufacturing personel in as much as there has been so much of it lately. Be there by 9:00 a.m. Have info ready on your people so we'll know who has been tardy and who hasn't been. We contumplate no punative action against aledge offenders at this time in so far as July is concerned. But August will be a different matter. Three tardy days and pay will be docked from offenders. The meeting will be in the conference room.

This man is inspecting welding work using the radiographic technique to determine hidden defects. He will be required to write a report of his findings.

CHAPTER 2

Building Sentences

A small baby expresses himself with a single method: he cries. He cries when he is hungry and he cries when he has pain. The remainder of his young life is spent either in sleeping or in quiet general contentment—with a few grunts and "goo-goo" sounds thrown in for good measure. As the child develops to the toddler stage, he learns individual words to express his desires: "ma-ma," when he wants attention or "milk," when he wants a drink. As a subteen, the child learns sentence values in expressing himself: "I want a drink of warm milk before bed." Now, he not only tells that he wants a drink of milk, but he can describe its desired quality and can state the time when he wants to drink it. So the process continues into adulthood.

You, as an adult, have many desires and needs. When you seek employment, you will need to write a letter requesting a job from a specific company. The company may ask that you prepare a resumé of your education, training, and experience. When you are employed, you will be asked to write reports on your technical specialty. If you are to purchase equipment and supplies, often you will be required to write letters requesting information from potential suppliers. If you are sent on a field trip, company management will request you to write a report of your activities. If you are self-employed you will need to write business letters and make bids for obtaining work. Thus, paperwork is a major part of vocational and business life.

As a person with a sound vocational background, you have much to offer an employer. But unless you can express yourself moderately well in writing, you will not be able to convince other people of your real abilities. On the other hand, if you can learn to put your thoughts in writing in a concise and clear manner, you will find satisfactory employment more readily and will advance to supervisory levels more rapidly. An employee who can write is much more valuable to a company than one who cannot.

What Is a Sentence?

A sentence is a unit of speech which expresses at least one complete thought. That thought must contain a subject and a verb. Some sentences can contain more than one complete (major) thought, and often contain incomplete (minor) thoughts as well. Sentences are classified in three ways: by *function*, *style*, and *structure*.

How Do Sentences Work? (Function)

A sentence can perform one of four general functions:

    (1) It can make a statement
    (2) It can ask a question
    (3) It can give a command
    (4) It can express strong feeling

Some examples include:

Making a Statement (Declarative):

    We will expect your firm to comply with the guarante.
    (The sentence ends with a period.)

Asking a Question (Interrogative):

    Will your firm comply with this guarantee?
    (The sentence ends with a question mark.)

Giving a Command (*Imperative*):

> Your firm will comply with this guarantee!
> (It may end with period or exclamation point.)

Expressing Strong Feeling (*Exclamatory*):

> We insist that you comply with this guarantee!
> (It always ends with an exclamation point.)

Technically, these four types of sentences are named the declarative, interrogative, imperative, and exclamatory forms. It is not important that you memorize these names, but you should be able to identify the four sentence types by stating their function.

What Is Sentence Style?

Style refers to the order of words in a sentence. This order usually follows three patterns, where main structure is at the beginning; main structure is at the end; or two main structures are present. Examples include:

Main Structure at Beginning (*Loose*):

> *main structure*
> The contract ended when the painting and clean-up work were completed.

Main Structure at End (*Periodic*):

> *main structure*
> After searching for several hours, we found your ammeter.

Two Equal Structures (*Parallel*):

> *main structure*　　　　　*main structure*
> The project foreman was dismissed; the assistant foreman was retained.

All these sentence styles may be used effectively in your writing.

How Are Sentences Constructed?

As previously mentioned, sentences can contain two kinds of thoughts:

Major thoughts, which can stand alone:
independent clause

The apprentice operated the lathe.

Minor thoughts, which cannot stand alone because their meaning is incomplete:

introductory
conjunction

Until the work   was completed

subject *verb*

Put together, this sentence reads:

The apprentice operated the lathe until the work was completed.

Or, it could read:
dependent clause

Until the work was completed, the apprentice operated the lathe.

In the above example, the minor thought came either before or after a major thought. Sometimes the minor thought can come in the middle of a major thought:

minor thought

The man who performs well will be hired.

introductory
pronoun

To determine whether a thought is *major* or *minor,* ask yourself if it will stand alone without any other explanation. If it won't stand, it is a minor thought.

Each minor thought will begin with an introductory conjunction or introductory pronoun.

Some Introductory Conjunctions:

since	when	after
until	if	because
before	although	unless

Some Introductory Pronouns:

whose	that	whoever
who	whatever	what
which	whom	

Sentences may take forms of construction ranging from the very simple to the very complicated. When you write, it is best to make your sentences as simple as possible, but you should also be aware of the basic construction techniques in writing the more complicated forms. Examples follow:

Sentences with One Major Thought (Simple Sentence):

major thought

The machinist turned 10 pieces.

subject   verb

Sentences with Two Major Thoughts (Compound Sentence):

major thought   major thought

The machinist turned 10 pieces and he sent them to be inspected.

conjunction

The machinist turned 10 pieces; he sent them to be inspected.

semicolon

Sentences with a Major and a Minor Thought (Complex Sentence):

major thought   minor thought

The apprentice operated the lathe until the work was completed.

introductory
conjunction

Sentences with Several Thoughts (Compound-Complex Sentence):

The machinist turned 10 pieces; he placed them on the shelf until they were inspected.

When the machinist was 30 years old, he developed a new procedure for lathe operation; this procedure saved Allen-Jones Steel Company $93,000 in a one-year test operation. (28 words)

Sentence Formula

Of course it is possible to write all short sentences—even a one-word sentence:

Come.
(with the subject "You" understood)

However, in vocational and industrial writing, it is most acceptable to write sentences from 15 to 25 words in length. In general, it is best to keep subjects near verbs, pronouns near their reference nouns, and modifiers near the word they modify.

Short sentences grouped together make the writing sound abrupt. At the other extreme, when faced with a series of long, complicated sentences, the reader will soon give up.

Sentences too Short:

> Most of the human body is water. Water acts as a solvent for many life-giving chemicals. These chemicals are the substances which permit life to occur. Without them, food digestion could not take place. (34 words)

Sentence too Long:

> Most of the human body is water, acting as a solvent for many chemicals which are life giving substances that are necessary for food digestion processes to occur. (28 words)

Sentences about Right:

> Most of the human body is water, which acts as a chemical solvent. Some of these dissolved chemicals are the life-giving substances which permit food digestion processes to occur. (29 words)

Better yet:

> Water comprises 80 percent of the human body and acts as a solvent for the life-giving biochemicals which permit food digestion to occur. (24 words)

Subject-Verb Relationships

Another common problem in sentence writing involves subject and verb *number relationships:*

> Portable power saws and other tools such as the half-inch drill *is* essential for efficient production.

Analysis:

Subjects: saws and tools (compound subjects)
Written verb: is (singular)
Correct verb: are (plural)

> A thorough knowledge of blueprint reading and associated space relationships *are* invaluable *tools* for the successful journeyman.

Analysis:

  Subject: knowledge (singular)
  Written verb: are (plural)
  Correct verb: is (singular)
  Correct subjective compliment: tool (singular)

To guard against such embarrassing errors, it is essential to read and review all subject verb number relationships while writing them.

Dangling Modifiers

  The plumbing installation requires a pressure reducing valve on this incomplete plan *to prevent line bursts and resultant structural damage.*

Analysis:

The italicized infinitive phrase is acting as an adjective and modifies the noun *valve*. The writer has interjected a prepositional phrase, *on this incomplete plan* between the noun and its modifying adjective—leaving the adjective phrase dangling.

Better:

  This incomplete plumbing plan requires a pressure reducing valve to prevent line bursts and resultant structural damage.

A Choice of Words

One of the most common problems in writing is caused by trying to say too much in one sentence. Remember that the fewer words you can use to adequately tell your story, the better the writing.

The use of clichés is prevalent in poor writing.

Example

  Insofar as our company is concerned, the performance of your resistors do not meet specifications *to say the least* and *after due consideration,* we are returning them to you *under separate cover.* (32 words)

Analysis:

Four unnecessary clichés are used (italicized). Too many words are used to say too little, and a wrong verb is used.

Better Writing:

> We have tested your resistors and found that they do not meet specifications. Therefore, we have shipped the remaining lots to you for a refund credit. (26 words saying much more)

The following list of clichés should be avoided in sentence writing:

inasmuch as	please feel free
insofar as	all in all
enclosed herewith is	to say the least
to a certain extent	by means of
to a certain degree	in the neighborhood of
here to with	under separate cover
as a matter of fact	we beg to advise
and the like	we beg to state
after due consideration	we beg to differ
needless to say	we beg to acknowledge
suffice it to say	I have before me
as per	I have in hand
in re(regard) to	I wish to say that
as nearly as	I wish to state
hanging in the balance	I would say
in this day and age	the fact of the matter is
the truth of the matter is	the sum of

Vague Pronoun References

Many writers exhibit a characteristic in their work called *vague pronoun references*. This fault occurs when a noun is written in a sentence between a subject noun and a pronoun reference:

> Damage can occur to the AC power unit when the *cover* is kept closed because of its sensitivity to heat. (20 words)

Analysis:

Does the pronoun *its* refer to *cover* or *unit?* The writer really wanted *it* to refer to the noun *unit*. In correcting this problem, the noun *cover* must be moved to another position in the sentence.

Improved Sentence:

> Because of its sensitivity to heat, damage can occur to the AC power unit when the cover is kept closed. (20 words)

But this sentence is still somewhat awkward and it lacks punch. Let's try again:

Additional Improvement:

> Heat can damage this AC power unit if the cover is kept closed. (13 words)

Balance or Symmetry

Lack of symmetry in company communications is not as common as many other problems, but it does occur frequently enough to need discussion. Consider this compound sentence:

> Mr. Smith resigned; Mr. Davis, Lead Machinist, and an old friend of the Smith family, was appointed to succeed him as General Manager.

Analysis:

To make this compound sentence perfectly symmetrical we would be forced to write:

> Mr. Smith, General Manager, resigned; Mr. Davis, Lead Machinist, succeeded him.

A Better Version:

> Mr. T. W. Smith, General Manager of Allen-Jones Steel Company, resigned his position, effective September 1, 19—; Mr. R. W. Davis, who is Lead Machinist in charge of production, was appointed to fill the vacant managerial post.

Notice in the improved version that additional knowledge about the situation was necessary before a more fluid and readable sentence could be written.

Sentence Repair

In each of the previous examples, an attempt was made to improve sentence construction. Just how was this done? The writer literally took the basic sentence elements apart (mentally) and reconstructed them in a different, more effective way. Sometimes clauses and phrases were rearranged within a sentence; sometimes one sentence was made from two, or two sentences were made from one; and sometimes an entirely new writing approach was necessary. Use of these techniques is the key to producing effective written communication.

EXERCISES

1. Identify subjects and verbs in the following sentences:

   a. Current flows through an electrical conductor because of electrical pressure.
   b. An electrician is expected to furnish his own hand tools.
   c. Pulling wire and making splices are the most time consuming parts of electrical installation.
   d. Sheet metal workers use scratch awls to mark lines on metals.
   e. A successful riveting operation depends upon the accuracy and size of the rivet holes and upon the correct size and spacing of the rivets.
   f. Light metal is punched; heavier metal is drilled.
   g. Soft solder is composed of tin and lead and its melting point largely depends upon the proportions of these two elements.
   h. Electrical resistance is the opposition of a conductor to the flow of electrons.

2. Identify the major and minor thoughts in the following sentences:

   a. The machinist turned 10 pieces; he placed them on the shelf until they were inspected.
   b. When the machinist was 30 years old, he developed a new procedure for lathe operation; this procedure saved Allen-Jones Steel Company $93,000 in a one year test program.

    c. Striking an arc and running a straight bead are basic operations in the skill of arc welding.

    d. Shielded electrodes for arc welding are coated with various substances which serve a particular function in the welding process.

    e. Because of its high cost, concrete formwork is often more important from an economical point of view than the concrete itself.

    f. Since one cubic foot of concrete weighs approximately 150 pounds, formwork must be heavily braced, thus preventing breaks and costly spills.

    g. The simplest form of waterproofing for foundations built in soil which is moderately damp, is to apply hot tar or asphalt to the outside surface.

    h. Although its chief function is now ornamental, the fireplace continues to be a part of the American home because of the informal, relaxed air it suggests.

3. Identify the following sentences according to style:

    a. He jumped down hard on the box, breaking it into several pieces.

    b. The machinist turned 10 pieces; he placed them on the inspection shelf.

    c. It was several hours until the error was found.

    d. The errors were discovered; however, it was too late to make any changes.

4. List the minimum and maximum number of words recommended for use in a sentence.

5. From a daily newspaper or magazine, clip two of the following types of sentences, and glue them on a piece of typing or notebook paper.

a. Give a command	g. Two equal structures
b. Ask a question	h. One major thought only
c. Make a statement	i. Two major thoughts only
d. Express strong feeling	j. Major and minor thought only
e. Main structure at beginning	k. Several (3 or more) thoughts
f. Main structure at end	

6. Diagnose and state what is wrong with each of the following sentences, and then rewrite each sentence in a better form:

   a. After due consideration, the machinist turned 1000 retaining rods for Allen-Jones steel company all at one time, which will save set-up time in the neighborhood of five percent after a lengthy evaluation of the results.

   b. "It'll be covered up anyway," is a common excuse for poor workmanship which we believe is bad thinking if you are to succeed in this craft.

   c. On the basis of past history we inaugurated this program to supply a superbly magnificent quality control program of which we are very proud.

   d. Enclosed herewith is a detailed report showing construction progress to date with which we are very pleased.

   e. We have enclosed the general contract for the approval of the manager for the manufacture of the electron tubes which are based on a precise specification with specified standards.

   f. A business meeting will be held Monday. It will be at 3:00 p.m. We will discuss technical info for the upcoming presentation in the company's annual stock meeting. Please be in attendance and bring all necessary support that you will require.

   g. Use of a 16-penny gun to drive nails in house framing is an excellent example of the use of hydraulic air compression principles.

   h. We installed a plenum chamber that did not permit insertion of a standard fiberglass air filter. So we are sorry and will come out to your house and correct the problem and also adjust the lighting of the furnace to prevent the chamber from expanding too rapidly and making the loud noise you complained about.

   i. Should a plumber wipe each soldered joint in copper tubing to provide a neat appearing connection while it is still hot or should he "gob" on the solder and hope the inspectors will pass the job?

   j. Which decision should we make on whether we should use copper or aluminum electrical wire in house construction?

7. Rewrite these sentences in three different, but effective ways:

   a. Damage can occur to the AC power unit when the cover is kept closed because of its sensitivity to heat.

b. Until tomorrow, the tests will not continue.
c. Insofar as our company is concerned, the performance of your resistors do not meet specifications.
d. The plumbing installation requires a pressure reducing valve on this incomplete plan to prevent line bursts and resultant structural damage to both the pipes and the concrete inner wall where the pipes are encased.

This young woman is learning to place components on electronic printed circuit boards by means of a new television training technique. She will be asked to evaluate the new teaching method by writing a critical report. (Videosonic Systems Division, Hughes Aircraft Company)

CHAPTER 3

Constructing a Paragraph

A paragraph consists of one or more sentences which present related thoughts about a subject. It is usually larger than a single sentence, yet usually smaller than an entire composition. Thus, a paragraph is an intermediate part of any composition.

Paragraph Forms

There are basically four paragraph types which may be employed:

(1) Paragraphs with no conclusion or a summary sentence
(2) Paragraphs with a conclusion or summary in the final sentence
(3) Paragraphs with a conclusion or summary at beginning
(4) Paragraphs with a conclusion in the middle

Paragraph with No Conclusion (Unresolved):

Example

To replace this defective electronic modular unit, first remove the outer cover of the case by turning counterclockwise the two locking wing nuts (marked A and B in Figure 1). This will release the outer cover and expose the inner cover. The inner cover is removed by releasing four slot-type screws (marked C in Figure 2). After the second cover is free, remove it entirely from the case to permit easy entry to the access hole.

In this paragraph, no single sentence is dominant. There is no conclusion or generalization made. Ordinarily, this type of paragraph is used in vocational, technical or business communications when writing instructions or descriptions.

Paragraph with Conclusion at End (Inductive):

Example

Printed circuit boards are more resistant to vibration damage than a wired chassis because components are soldered to the boards by the new mass-flow techniques. They can be miniaturized more extensively than those produced by hand soldering. Printed circuits are also less expensive to manufacture because they eliminate the laborious task of hand soldering. *Therefore, we should investigate the feasibility of using these boards in our computer manufacturing process.*

The paragraph with conclusion at the end presents a series of statements and then draws a conclusion in the final sentence. This form of discussion is comparable to the form of a formal argument (syllogism) discussed in Chapter I, and is *very effectively used* in summarizing the results of an investigation or study.

Paragraph with Conclusion at Beginning (Deductive):

Example

The printed circuit board is more reliable than the old solder-and-wire chassis. Human assembly errors are eliminated because the boards are made entirely by mechanical means. In addition, the printed circuits are highly resistant to vibration damage because handmade wire-solder connections have been replaced by new mass-flow soldering techniques.

A summary or general statement is made in the first sentence of the above paragraph. Then the paragraph expands on the subject by relating detailed support information in the sentences that follow. This paragraph style is the most common and useful form in use by modern writers. In your work, you should have many paragraphs with the main thoughts written first.

Paragraph with Conclusion in Middle (Inductive-Deductive):

Example

Printed circuit boards can be miniaturized more readily than those electrical circuits produced by hand soldering methods. Human assembly errors are eliminated because the boards are made entirely by mechanical means. *Therefore, we should consider the feasibility of using these boards in our computer manufacturing process.* Our labor costs would be reduced greatly and many of our quality control problems eliminated. In addition, miniaturization could reduce greatly the bulk size of our computer units.

This paragraph form begins with at least one statement, draws a conclusion (see the italicized sentence in the example above), and then continues with more sentences on the effects of the conclusion. In most such writing, this paragraph form should be avoided, because it is usually too complex for effective communication. The example given above might be better written in a paragraph with the summary at the beginning as shown below:

We should consider the feasibility of using printed circuit boards in our computer manufacturing process. These printed circuits can be miniaturized more readily than those produced with hand soldering methods, therefore the bulk size of our computer units could be greatly reduced. Circuit reliability would be improved because human assembly errors are eliminated by mechanical manufacturing techniques. In addition, estimates show that some manufacturing labor costs would be reduced.

Paragraph Formula

There is no such thing as a paragraph formula that fits all writing situations. However, the most effective written communication originates from paragraphs that are from 50 to 75 words in length. Usually this means that paragraphs should contain 3 to 6 sentences. These rules are based on the following facts:

(1) Short, choppy paragraphs tend to irritate the reader and may cause him to lose the thread of the argument.

(2) Long, involved paragraphs tend to tire the reader, and he will soon give up the painful task of trying to determine the meaning. For example, if a paragraph leads off with a general statement followed up by a dozen sentences explaining detail, the reader will often forget the main thought and must reread the paragraph to determine the relationship between the main thought and the ninth sentence.

(3) People expect paragraphs to be 50 to 75 words in length. To most readers this length is bite size. When confronted with long, short, or unusual paragraphs, the reader finds himself paying more attention to the different writing style than he does to the meaning.

Transitions Between Sentences and Paragraphs

An important factor in consecutive paragraph (and sentence) development is the effective use of transitional words:

first later thereafter then now	indicate time and sequence relationships
therefore accordingly consequently thus unfortunately	indicate a cause relationship
in the upper left below above overhead in the foreground	indicate space relationships
but and however nevertheless further furthermore in addition	indicate qualifications

Example

We have investigated your complaint that 160 M-123A tubes were damaged during shipment and arrived at your firm in an unusable condition. *Unfortunately,* a retaining band in the shipping van broke, resulting in the reported damage.

Therefore, a new order has been sent via the same transport firm (Husky Trucking Co.), with arrival scheduled for March 4. Cost of the shipment will be paid by Husky Trucking Company.

In the preceding example, two (italicized) transition words were used. One begins a sentence and the other begins a paragraph. Read the above paragraphs over again as though the transition words simply were not there. The paragraphs still make sense but are probably not as effective. Without effective use of transitional words, the entire intent of a discussion can occasionally be lost.

When to Start a New Paragraph

Faulty paragraphing is a common problem with many writers. So how do you know when to start a new paragraph? Again, there are no firm rules, but these suggestions should help: Unless you are writing descriptions or instructions, each paragraph should contain a general or summary statement at the beginning. Sometimes one-sentence paragraphs are both essential and effective. Normally, however, it's best not to write paragraphs shorter than two sentences or longer than six. Generally, complicated subjects require longer paragraphs than simpler ones.

What's wrong with the paragraphing in this business letter, and how do you correct it?

Husky Trucking Co. will deliver 160 reams of 60 pound 8½″ x 11″ No. 14 opaque offset printing paper to your receiving dock on or before October 1. Unfortunately, a retaining band in our van accidentally came loose during shipment, resulting in damage to your paper. We will expect to receive payment for the entire shipment (bill of lading No. 2163) upon satisfactory delivery of the 160 reams. If this band had not slipped, your paper would have arrived in satisfactory condition. Husky Trucking Co. wishes to apologize for any inconvenience that this loss may

have caused. We will pay the cost of supplying the new paper.
We regard Jaffa Printing Company as one of our finest customers and we are anticipating a continuing successful business
relationship between our firms. (131 words)

Analysis:

This paragraph, which discusses a relatively simple subject,
is too long; the sentences are not in a correct and logical
sequence. Too many words are used to say too little. This
letter should be rewritten in two or three paragraphs.

Corrective Action:

First, try to determine a good lead sentence for the first
paragraph. (Often, there is more than one good sentence that
could be used.)

After the first sentence has been selected, follow with those
sentences in the same paragraph that explain or modify the
lead sentence. Then, go to a second paragraph and select a
new lead sentence. Follow up by writing in the same paragraph
those sentences that are associated with that lead thought.

Continue this process until you have said all that needs to
be said.

Remember that some sentences may require modification to
meet changes in the new paragraph groupings.

Improved Paragraphing, Using Same Sentences:

Unfortunately, a retaining band accidentally came loose in
our delivery van—resulting in damage to your paper. If this
band had not slipped, your paper would have arrived in satisfactory condition.

Husky Trucking Co. will deliver 160 reams of 60 8½″ x 11″
No. 14 opaque offset printing paper to your receiving dock on or
before October 1. We will pay the cost of supplying the new
paper. We will expect to receive payment for the entire shipment (bill of lading No. 2163) upon satisfactory delivery of the
160 reams.

Husky Trucking Co. wishes to apologize for any inconvenience
that this loss may have caused. We regard Jaffa Printing Company as one of our finest customers, and we are anticipating a
continuing successful business relationship between our firms.´
(still 128 words)

The above letter revision is probably adequate, and it typifies the average business letter. However, by rearranging some sentences or fragments, and by taking away and adding a few elements this letter can be improved further:

Letter Improved by Rearranging, Adding and Eliminating:

> Unfortunately, 160 reams of 60-pound 8½" x 11" No. 14 opaque offset printing paper were damaged while en route to your firm. A replacement supply will be delivered to your receiving department before October 2, at no cost to you.
>
> Husky Trucking Co. apologizes for any inconvenience this loss may have caused. Jaffa Printing Company is one of our finest customers, and we are anticipating a continuing successful business relationship between our firms. (72 words)

But haven't we left out some important parts of the initial draft? We didn't explain how the paper was damaged. And, we didn't ask for payment. Well, Jaffa Printing Company probably doesn't care how the paper was damaged. Further, it is not proper to request immediate payment in a letter of apology.

Could we improve this letter further? Probably. But further overwriting would simply require more time and money and would not provide any worth while results. How do you know when to quit? When the writing says what you want it to say —with good grammar, with good arrangement of thoughts, and with a minimum amount of words. When you've done your best, quit!

EXERCISES

1. Define the term *paragraph*.

2. Identify the concluding or general statement (if there is one) in each of the following paragraphs.

   a. It is common in the building trades for a man to work his way up the ladder of responsibility from apprentice to contractor—staying at each level until he is proficient. When a craftsman decides to become a contractor, he must prepare himself for operating under a whole new set of

.rules and conditions. As a contractor, he will be risking his own money on the gamble that his knowledge and experience in estimating work, handling men and keeping up with the paperwork that is required today will pay a profit. With these factors understood, the new contractor stands ready to bid against his fellow contractors on the work that is available.

b. Gypsum lath is now made in a number of sizes, thicknesses, and types, with each type used for a specific purpose or condition. Only gypsum mortar can be used over gypsum lath. Never apply lime mortar, portland cement or any other binding agent to gypsum lath.

c. As more complicated automobiles appear on the road, with such refinements as automatic transmissions, power steering, power breaks, and high compression engines, the demand for skilled mechanics has increased. It is no longer very practical for unskilled owners to repair their own machines. Without men properly trained for motor vehicle service, our automotive system would soon collapse.

d. A differential unit in the rear axle assembly permits the rear wheels to rotate at different speeds when the vehicle turns a corner. If the vehicle were always driven in a straight line, a differential would not be necessary. When the vehicle makes a turn, however, the outside wheel must turn faster than the inside wheel to prevent skidding or excessive tire wear.

e. The sealed beam headlamp consists of a lens, a glass reflector with an aluminum reflecting surface deposited on its inner surface, and one or two filaments assembled into a permanently sealed unit. During assembly, the unit is filled with an inert gas. Because the unit is sealed against dirt, moisture, and corrosion, there is little decrease in the amount of projected light throughout its life.

f. A leaky automobile fuel tank can sometimes be repaired by soldering. Unfortunately, however, soldering a fuel tank is a dangerous job, and extreme caution must be used to avoid an explosion. Even an empty fuel tank can explode as readily as a tank containing fuel. Because passenger car fuel tanks are generally not expensive, it is often advisable to replace a leaky tank with a new one rather than to repair it.

g. Regardless of the type of bacteria that can spoil food, all grow very rapidly under favorable conditions. Favorable conditions include warmth and moisture. With this knowledge, food service personnel must make certain that these conditions do not exist when storing or preparing foods. Bacteria is present in all foods so the chief weapon against these germs is temperature control through refrigeration or cooking; dry food must be stored under dry conditions.

h. Specifications are a vital part of the building plans. They give additional details to the information shown on drawings or blueprints. They contain written instructions with necessary information pertaining to types of materials to be used, fabrication and installation techniques, colors, quality of finishes and other details.

i. After the wiring is pulled into place on a construction job, all wire-to-wire connections or splices are made. The first step in making any kind of wire connection is to remove the insulation. For this purpose, use a sharp knife. Do not circle the wire with the blade at right angles, because in most cases this produces a groove in the conductor which may cause the wire to break when it is bent at this point. A groove may also reduce the capacity of the wire to carry current. Instead, whittle the insulation away in a manner similar to that of sharpening a pencil, at an angle of about 30 degrees.

3. From newspaper and magazines, clip out six of each of the following paragraph forms and glue them on a piece of typing or notebook paper.

a. Paragraph with general statement at beginning.
b. Paragraph with general statement at end.
c. Paragraph with general statement in middle.
d. Paragraph with no general statement.

Please note that you may have difficulty in locating pure examples of paragraphs with no general statement or with general statement in the middle.

4. Write paragraphs with general statement at the beginning on four of these topics:

a. House framing
b. Television tube function
c. Spark plug performance
d. Chain saw operation
e. H_2SO_4
f. Sweat soldering copper pipe
g. Forced-air duct work
h. Btu
i. Transit operation

j. Use of a carpenter's square
k. Metric system units
l. Concrete strength factors
m. Drafting table operation
n. Magnetic recording tape
o. Printed circuit boards
p. Solder
q. Mixing mortar
r. Plumb bob use

Don't be afraid to do a little investigative work so you'll know what you're talking about.

5. Now, rewrite the paragraphs that you prepared in exercise 4 so the general statement is at the end.

6. Use your own reasoning to rewrite the following letters:

No. 1

Husky Trucking Co. will deliver 160 reams of 60 lb 8½" x 11" No. 14 opaque offset printing paper to replace part of the previous shipment that was damaged while enroute to you. It will arrive at your receiving dock on or before October 1. Unfortunately, a retaining band, in our van, accidentally broke during shipment, resulting in damage to your paper. We don't expect payment at this time for the entire shipment, but will bill you at a later date. Husky Trucking Co. wishes to apologize for any inconvenience that this loss may have caused. We really do regard Jaffa Printing Company as one of our finest customers, and we definitely are anticipating a fabulous, successful business relationship between our two great firms.

No. 2

You are correct! We have overcharged your account in the amount of $197.63

This accounting error resulted because of the similarity between your name and that of another customer. The other Smith Electronics should have been charged with this $197.63, but somehow the girl punched the wrong code into our computer. Would you like a cash refund or would you like the amount credited to your account as a plus balance for future purchases?

Pleace accept our apology for this error; we have enclosed a new corrected June statement. Call us at once if there are any other problems concerned with your account.

No. 3

Allen-Jones Steel Company takes pride in meeting delivery schedules. As president of Allen-Jones Steel Company, I wish to thank you, Mr. Alton, for your recent order of 10 thousand stainless steel retaining rings. Because we meet nearly all of our delivery schedules, you can expect your first shipment of 500 units to arrive on December 20, 19— via Husky Trucking Co. In addition, additional shipments are scheduled to arrive on time on the twentieth of each month until final delivery is made in August. If I may be of further service to you, please call me at once by telephone at 373-0812, ext. 535.) It has been a pleasure to serve your fine firm in the past years, and it is hoped that our excellent business relationships will continue in the future.

7. You have a technical specialty in which you are interested. Write three paragraphs on the elements of success required of people in your field.

Installation of the duct work for this forced air heating system is behind schedule. The foreman in charge will be asked to write a report explaining the reasons for this delay.

CHAPTER 4

The Approach

Reports and other vocational writing require a simple and clear composition style. This reflects the increasing need for efficient, streamlined methods of operation in industry. Further, it is a recognition that writing is more effective when it is easy to read.

Too many writers have been slow in adopting the more modern styles. Some continue to lean on tired, standard phrases and old fashioned styles inherited from years ago. These weak forms of writing are used by some because the style is believed to be official or impressive. Neither should be the reason for selecting an approach to writing a report.

The correct method or manner of writing is selected because it fits the subject matter, the reader, and the writer. Thus, the general purposes of stylistic method are to:

(1) Promote rapid reading
(2) State the exact meaning
(3) Show restraint
(4) Be objective
(5) Be clear for future reference

As previously mentioned, cost-consciousness about report writing is important. The cost of writing, reproducing, distributing, reading, and filing a single page in an organization is measured in tens or hundreds of dollars. Further, most people who read reports have limited time. The writer, then, must consider these points and prepare a document that *promotes rapid reading*.

In a report, the message must be clear to the reader. The entire effort of preparing and reading a report is wasted if the style fails to *state the exact meaning*.

The report writer's enthusiasm must be controlled. Bragging and other exaggerations are out of place in a document that is to state the truth without unnecessary words. The loud language of advertising and public relations is out of place in most reports. The style, therefore, must *show restraint*.

The emphasis in a report is seldom on the writer. The emphasis is placed on the truth about what occurred and what was observed. Thus, the style must *be objective*.

Most reports are filed for later use. The report must *be inclusive enough to be clear for future reference*.

The Tone of Vocational Writing

As noted in the previous section, the proper writing approach requires objectivity by the writer. The emphasis is upon the facts. Usually the writer who is employed as a specialist to conduct an investigation and write a report should have an impartial attitude toward the work. Likewise, the written material resulting from the investigation will be impersonal in tone. This, however, may not be true when the writer has a personal interest in the results of the report or if the readers are well known by the writer. The writer may then use a considerably more informal style.

But always keep in mind that objectivity and the lack of personal attitudes have long been characteristics of good technical communications.

Making the Report Fit the Reader

The need for making a report suit the interest, knowledge, and desires of the reader is suggested in the prior sections. This adaptation to the reader and the relationship with the purpose of a report deserves more consideration, however, than just a suggestion. Regardless of the excellence in composition, the report is useless if it does not speak to the reader.

Readers differ considerably in ability to understand and to use a given report. Yet, the writer communicates effectively only when the material is presented in a manner that the reader understands easily. This ability to understand depends upon the reader's experience—not on the writer's. Vocational and technical terms and abbreviations may be used when the reader has such a background; but if the report is intended for a nontechnical person, such terms and abbreviations are certainly out of place.

A report intended only for managers with similar backgrounds is written in the language of that field. The terms, phrases, and abbreviations used in the report are common knowledge among this group of readers. A further explanation of the terms is not necessary. However, a report on the same subject, addressed to people with general interest backgrounds, should be written in a style to fit the different readership.

When trying to analyze human beings there are many chances for making mistakes. These dangers are even greater when trying to analyze readers whom the writer may not know very well. In such circumstances, the writer is almost certain to overestimate or underestimate the knowledge of some of the readers.

Still, a report writer must assess the readership. Specific information about an individual is worth much more than a general classification of a reader as technical or nontechnical, for example. One reader prefers bare facts; another wants every minute detail reported. Some readers not only want the material to be interesting but expect it to be entertaining.

It is not within the scope of this book to try to comment on all the differences among readers. Commonly, however, these differences are in:

(1) Education, special training, job and experience
(2) Background information needed to help the reader understand the subject
(3) The detail required to satisfy the reader's needs
(4) Ability to understand abbreviations, symbols, visual aids, and references to laws of science, or principles of industrial production
(5) Personality and preferences for a particular style
(6) The purpose for which the report will be used

To be effective, the writer must try to see the problems associated with each reader.

Effective Writing

In spite of many differences, there are well-founded qualities that help the writer achieve the desired communication effects. These are:

(1) Thoroughness
(2) Directness
(3) Conciseness
(4) Clearness
(5) Concreteness
(6) Consistency

Thoroughness. Successful writers know that deciding what to leave out of a report is almost as important as deciding what should be included. Words, ideas, or facts that are not necessary to the understanding only weaken the report. It is the writer's job, of course, to determine exactly how much of the available information should be included. The problem is usually too much material rather than too little. The task, then, is often one of defining the purpose of the report and discarding useless material.

It is essential, however, that a report be comprehensive enough that the reader will not need to ask important questions about the report's contents. If the following questions are not answered, the information is usually incomplete:

Who? Individuals and organizations involved in the report should be identified. *Who* conducted the research or study, *who* evaluated the data, *who* reached the conclusions, and *who* made the recommendations are important to the reader. This is especially true when the reader must make decisions based upon the information in the report, often involving additional work and expenses. Knowing *who* performed the various tasks presented in the report can be the key to the final decision. Also, when further action or a decision is required, the writer should specify *who* is to take the action or make the decision. Otherwise, the desired results of the report may never be achieved.

What? Facts which give details of the situation and its consequences are essential in a report that can be called complete. Only the significant facts are needed to ensure this completeness, though. It is seldom necessary to include all the facts that have been gathered. It is important, however, that the reader be given enough facts to understand *what* was done and the results obtained.

When? The time sequence involved should be specified. Often it is important that the reader know not only the overall time span but when each event took place or will take place. In many instances, knowing *when* certain steps were taken ties the whole report together.

Where? The location involved should be described. Depending upon the type of report and the situation, this could be a relatively minor or a major part of a report. It is not necessary, for example, to give a detailed description of a location in a progress report that deals with tasks being performed over a period of time in a certain laboratory or plant. Such a description is often provided in documents submitted prior to the beginning of the actual work on the project. In the progress report the location may need to be only generally identified. However, a report on a building program would probably require an extensive description of the area and facilities.

Why? Informative writing is made more understandable by an explanation of *why* something is done. The writer should explain the reasons for the sequence of events described in the report. If the general purpose of a report is to persuade someone to take action, *why* this action is needed becomes the vital part of the document.

How? Exactly *how* something is done is often the nucleus of a report. In fact, the sole purpose of many reports is to tell the reader how something is accomplished. This is where detail becomes obviously important to the reader and thus to the report writer. To specify the wrong material or to list procedures out of proper sequence could be a costly and possibly a dangerous error. Therefore, the part of the report that includes these steps deserves the writer's serious attention.

Directness. The writer should come to the point as quickly as possible. Time should not be wasted on unimportant preliminary details. When possible, begin each paragraph with general statements and then develop it by stating details. (See Chapter 3.)

The report writer does not try to keep the reader guessing. The questions are answered and the necessary details are presented to explain the answer.

Conciseness. The report writer should make certain that each word, each statement, and each point is important enough to include. The lengthy report is certainly not always the best one. In fact, often a lengthy report means that the writer has not taken the time to go over it carefully, crossing out needless words, sentences, even paragraphs. (See Chapter 11, *Editing and Proofreading Techniques.*)

One hazard of a long report is that it may be scanned lightly and placed aside, or it may never be read at all. Obviously the writer has failed in conveying the message when this happens.

The report writer has an obligation to save the reader's time. Most people in responsible jobs already spend a large part of the day reading material. An additional mass of unnecessary words is not wanted.

Conversely, a concerted effort to be too concise may result in a concentrated style that is difficult to understand. The writer should be thrifty—not stingy. The *essential* information must not be discarded.

Clearness. The report should be planned so that it will be in a logical order and easy to follow. Directness, thoroughness, and conciseness are essential in constructing clear sentences and paragraphs in a report. Good organization of sections is also important for clarity.

One of the great barriers to quick understanding is the unnecessary use of complex or unusual words. Often the writer who uses such words resorts to definitions. It is true that the writer should constantly guard against leaving important matters unexplained, but overuse of definitions only clogs the composition. The use of words that the reader readily understands makes definitions unnecessary.

Concreteness. Complicated and difficult words should be avoided in reports. Concrete words, which symbolize things that can be detected by the five senses, should be used instead.

The report writer, whenever possible, uses verifiable measurements—numbers and units—to make concrete statements. For example, the terms *large* and *small* are translated into measurements. Use of specific statements answers the reader's questions.

Consistency. Consistency is important to the reader's understanding of a report. It also saves the reader's time.

Failure to use the same specific term or name when referring to an event or an object often makes the composition difficult or impossible to understand. For example, don't use the term *static firing* first and later refer to the same event as a *static test.*

Consistency in the use of abbreviations, symbols, page numbering, headings, and other features of a report is also important for understanding and saving of reading time.

Abbreviations

Modern communications are often filled with confusing, troublesome abbreviations which cloud the meaning. For example, does anyone know what FICA really means? Of course we know it's a federal tax on wages, but few people know what words the letters represent. So why use abbreviations at all? Why not spell everything out each time? Abbreviations are used primarily because they save time and space. But to be effective, the reader must know their meaning. If the following rules are observed, you will find little trouble with the use of abbreviations in your writing.

(1) Use *only* singular abbreviations regardless of the situation.

Yes	*No*
in. lb sec	ins. lbs secs

(2) Normally, place a period after an abbreviation *only* if it spells a word.[1]

Period Required:		*No Period:*
in.	No.	msec lb ft
cat.		m ml cgs
a.m., p.m. (for consistency)		mil

Exception: Latin words, e.g., i.e., etc.

---

[1]In the latest American National Standard Institute publication on abbreviations ("Letter Symbols for Units Used in Science and Technology," ANSI Y10.19—1969) periods have been consistently dropped in all cases. ANSI Y1.1—1972, "Abbreviations for Use on Drawings and in Text," also follows this approach. If a report is to be written in a style to conform to the ANSI recommendations, reference should be made to

(3) Spell out uncommon abbreviations the first time they are used:

Mr. J. R. Smith is a past president of the American Institute of Electrical Engineers (AIEE).

With subsequent use, in that same report the abbreviation may be employed alone:

The AIEE is one . . .

(4) Always use letter abbreviations and avoid the use of symbols in their place:

Yes	*No*
lb, No., and	#, #, &

Exceptions: @ for at; 10°F for 10 deg F; " for in.; ' for ft.

(5) In most cases, capital letters are used for abbreviations that represent words which are capitalized in ordinary usage:

FCC—Federal Communications Commission

Btu—British thermal unit

There are exceptions:

No. by custom, to prevent confusion with word *no*.

mRNA, DNA—organic chemical compounds

Cl, N, etc.—chemical elements

V, KV, Hz—electrical abbreviations

(6) Do not begin a sentence with an abbreviation.

A valuable list of abbreviations is presented in Webster's latest *New Collegiate Dictionary* and in most other desk type dictionaries.

Numbers

Although not as pesky as abbreviations, numbers do cause some writers trouble. These rules are suggested to overcome the more common problems:

---

these two publications. (In addition, MIL STD 100, "Drawing Requirements Manual," gives a variant style for abbreviations which should be followed if the report is to be consistent to that style.)

(1) When citing units of measure, always use an Arabic number instead of spelling it out.

Yes	*No*
1″ long	One inch long
3.5 kcal/m²	Three and one-half kcal/m²

(2) Try to use decimal numbers *if possible* instead of fractional units:

Yes	*No*
3.5 kcal/m²	3-1/2 kcal/m²

But: ¼″ electric drill, not 0.25″ electric drill, unless all units are in decimals.

(3) When writing decimal numbers less than 1.0, place a 0 in front of the decimal.

Yes	*No*
0.396	.396

(4) When writing extremely large or small numbers on scientific subjects, use scientific notation form.

Yes	*No*
3.5×10^5	350,000
3.5×10^{-5}	0.000035

(5) Use commas in numbers 10,000 and above.

Yes	*No*
1,000,000	5,000
100,000	9,999
10,000	10000
9999	
5000	

Correct Usage of Terms

In this section, a glossary for some commonly misused and overworked words and sets of words is presented for review.

An effort has been made to list words often used in report writing. For more complete definitions and usages, a suitable dictionary should be consulted.

a, an	*A* should be used before all words beginning with a consonant sound, including *h* (if h is sounded).

Examples:

a hotel	an hour
a history	an ending

about, around	*About* means approximately. *Around* means circumference, or beginning at a point and returning to the same point.
above, above mentioned	*Above* should not be used as a noun. *Above mentioned* is overworked and awkward. The subject should be repeated or a synonym should be used.
accent, ascend ascent, assent	*Accent* is a verb (or related noun) meaning to emphasize.

Example: The scientist, to *accent* the importance of the tests, presented the entire plan.

Ascend is a verb meaning to climb or to rise.

Example: As the rocket began to *ascend*, the computer failure occurred.

Ascent is a noun meaning a rising.

Example: The rocket's *ascent* was made as programmed.

Assent is a verb (or related noun) meaning to agree.

Example: The supervising engineer gave immediate *assent* to the proposal.

accept, except	*Accept* means to receive or to approve. *Except* (as a verb) means to leave out.
accessible, assessable	*Accessible* is an adjective meaning reachable. Example: The bolt is *accessible* through the rear panel.
	Assessable is also an adjective meaning that which can be evaluated. Example: The property is *assessable* for tax purposes at any time.
adapt, adept, adopt	*Adapt* means to make fit or to adjust. Example: The astronaut will quickly *adapt* to the environment.
	Adept means skilled. Example: The technician is *adept* at controlling the flow of liquid.
	Adopt means to formally accept or to use. Example: The agreement was to *adopt* the plan if the tests were successful.
adhesion, cohesion	*Adhesion* means the union of unlike substances. Example: The *adhesion* of the wood to the plastic parts was made without difficulty.
	Cohesion means the union of similar substances. Example: The molecular *cohesion* of the new material was greater than the developers expected.

advice, advise, inform	*Advice* is a noun meaning suggestion. Example: It was upon the *advice* of the scientist that the tests were delayed. *Advise* is a verb meaning to suggest. Example: The evaluation group will *advise* management after the series of tests. *Inform* is also a verb meaning to make known. Example: The test engineer will *inform* the evaluation group of the results.
affect, effect	*Affect* should always be used as a verb. It means to influence. Example: The rain will *affect* the work on the project. *Effect* is usually a noun meaning result. Example: This is the effect of a well-planned project. *Effect* can also be used as a verb meaning to cause. Example: Pre-ignition was *effected* by a dangling wire.
all ready, already	*All ready* means wholly ready or completely prepared. Example: The equipment was *all ready*. *Already* means before a particular time. Example: The first step of the procedure had *already* been taken.
alternative, choice	*Alternative* refers to two only. Example: The *alternative* is to cancel the experiment. *Choice* refers to two or more. Example: One of the scientists' several *choices* is to cancel the experiment.

among, between	*Among* is used when referring to more than two persons or things. Example: The small engines were among the first ten to be shipped. *Between* is used when referring to only two persons or things. Example: The greatest difference in results is *between* the first two experiments.
amount, number	*Amount* is used when discussing things in bulk or mass. Example: The *amount* of water in the reservoir was measured. *Number* is used with persons or things that can be counted. Example: The *number* of people who observed the landing was unexpected.
antennae, antennas	*Antennae* is the plural form of a noun meaning feelers of an insect. *Antennas* is also a plural noun meaning more than one antenna.
as, like	*As* is used when a verb follows. Example: The tasks were performed *as* specified in the instructions. *Like* is used when no verb follows. Example: These instructions are *like* the others in many respects.
as per, as, since because	*As per* is meaningless; *according to* or a synonym should be used. The weak and often ambiguous use of *as* for *since* or *because* should be avoided. Example: The building was evacuated *because* (not *as*) the fire was beginning to spread.

attendance, attendants	*Attendance* means the act of being present. Example: The *attendance* of the chief engineer was unexpected. *Attendants* is a plural noun referring to those who care for. Example: There were *attendants* present to monitor the temperature.
balance, remainder	*Balance* should be used when referring to equilibrium, or a figure on a financial document. Example: The *balance* between the two compounds must be maintained throughout the process. *Remainder* refers to that which is left. Example: The *remainder* of the project will be completed next week.
beside, besides	*Beside* means at the side of, or close to. *Besides* means also or in addition to.
biannual, biennial, semiannual	*Biannual* and *semiannual* mean twice a year. *Biennial* means every two years.
bimonthly, biweekly,	*Bimonthly* means once every two months. *Biweekly* means once every two weeks.
semimonthly, semiweekly	*Semimonthly* means twice a month. *Semiweekly* means twice a week.
can, may	*Can* denotes ability. *May* denotes permission.
capacity, rating	*Capacity* means the measured ability to contain.

Rating means the stated operating limit. An engine's *rating*, for example, is usually lower than its *capacity*.

center, middle

Center is the point equidistant from the exterior points of a circle or sphere. *Middle* refers to a point or plane equidistant from the sides of a square or rectangle.

cite, site, sight

Cite is a verb meaning to refer to.
Example: Always *cite* the exact dimensions.
Site is a noun that means a location.
Example: The two final tasks are to be performed at the launching *site*.
Sight is used either as a noun or a verb. As a noun it means something that is seen, or a device used in aiming.
Example: The missile was tracked by *sight* during the first few moments after launch.
As a verb, *sight* means to take aim.
Example: The test engineer should *sight* the target before arming the device.

coarse, course

Coarse refers to relatively large parts or particles.
Course refers to a certain route.

comprise, compose

Comprise means to consist of or to include.
Compose means to form by putting something together.

continual, continuous

Continual means repeated frequently.
Example: There was a *continual* backfire from the engine.
Continuous means repeated without interruption.

Example: The static from the amplifier was *continuous*.

data
: *Data* is plural. The singular form, *datum,* is seldom used.
Example: The *data* are available immediately after the tests.

decent, descend, descent, dissent
: *Decent* means conforming to standards, or appropriate conduct.
Example: The offer was not considered *decent* by most of the participants.
Descend means to move downward.
Example: The technician was to *descend* through the opening.
Descent refers to the act of moving downward.
Example: The *descent* was made through a narrow passageway.
Dissent refers to a difference of opinion.
Example: The *dissent* was obvious to everyone present.

device, devise
: *Device* is a noun that refers to something contrived.
Devise is a verb that means to form or invent.

different from, different than
: *Different from* should be used. *Different than* is incorrect.

discover, invent
: Something that already exists is *discovered*. Something that is *invented* did not previously exist.

due to, because of
: *Due to* should not be used as an adverb in place of *because of*. *Due to* may, however, be used in the sense of assignable to.

Example: The malfunction was *due to* the rising temperature.

energy, force, work

Energy refers to the ability to perform work.

Force refers to the product of mass times acceleration.

Work refers to the product of the applied force and the distance a body is moved.

engine, motor

An *engine* is a device that transforms energy, especially thermal energy, into mechanical work. A gasoline *engine* is an example.

A *motor* is a device that uses an outside source of energy to perform mechanical work. An electric *motor* is an example.

ensure, insure

Ensure refers to making certain or making inevitable.

Insure refers to making secure.

envelop, envelope

Envelop is a verb that means to surround.

Envelope is a noun that means container.

farther, further

Farther should be used when expressing comparisons of physical distance.

Further should be used for other comparisons.

fewer, less

Fewer should be used when referring to number.

Less should be used when referring to amount.

fix, repair

Fix means to make immobile or firm.

	Repair means to restore to a suitable condition.
fluid, liquid	These words should not be used interchangeably. All *fluids* are not *liquids*.
gas, gasoline	*Gas* is a state of matter, which, because of its low density, tends to expand indefinitely, occupying the total volume of any vessel in which it is held. *Gasoline* is a liquid hydrocarbon mixture used as a fuel.
height, thickness	*Height* refers to the distance above a horizontal plane. *Thickness* refers to the distance beyond a frontal, vertical plane.
infra, ultra	*Infra* is a prefix that means below. *Ultra* is a prefix that means beyond what is ordinary.
in order to, to	*In order to* is overworked and awkward. *To* should be used instead.
inside of, within	*Inside of* should not be used in place of *within* when referring to time relationship.
lay, lie	*Lay* means to set down or to deposit. *Lie* means to rest or to be in a certain location.
many, much	*Many* should be used when referring to countable quantities. *Much* should be used when referring to bulk quantities.
mass, weight	*Mass* means the amount of matter con-

tained in a body. *Mass* is also used when referring to the resistance of a body to change of motion.

Weight means the force that results from gravitational attraction.

material, materiel

Material refers to the items used in performing a task.

Materiel refers to the supplies, equipment, and apparatus used by an organization.

maximum,
optimum (adj)

Maximum is defined as the greatest in value attainable in a given case.

Optimum is defined as the most favorable toward a certain goal.

mean, median,
mode

Mean refers to the arithmetic average and is commonly called the average.

Median refers to a point at which half of the items are the same as or smaller and half are the same as or larger than it.

Mode refers to the value around which the items tend to concentrate.

most, almost

Most should not be used for *almost* in the sense of nearly.

a number,
the number

A number usually refers to several persons or things, thus requiring a plural verb.

Example: *A number* of drawings are now available.

The number usually refers to a total and takes a singular verb.

Example: *The number* of personnel has increased.

percent, percentage	*Percent* should be used only with a number. Example: Eighty *percent* had been delivered. *Percentage* should never be used with a number. Example: A large *percentage* of the items had been delivered.
perform, preform	*Perform* means to carry out. *Preform* means to make beforehand.
perpendicular, vertical	*Perpendicular* refers to intersecting at a right angle. *Vertical* means perpendicular to the plane of the horizon or to a prime axis.
practicable, practical	*Practicable* should be used when referring to something that is capable of being put into practice. *Practical* means sensible when applied to persons and efficient when applied to things.
pressure, torque	*Pressure* is the force exerted per unit of area. *Torque* refers to the product of force and the lever arm in setting a body in rotation.
principal, principle	*Principal* conveys the idea of chief whether it is used as an adjective or as a noun. *Principle* is always a noun, meaning a general truth or a fixed rule.
range, vary	*Range* means the limits of a series. *Vary* means to make a partial change.

reliability, validity	*Reliability* refers to the possibility of obtaining the same results in repeated attempts. *Validity* refers to the probability that the measured variable is the variable being sought.
sewage, sewerage	*Sewage* refers to the waste matter (effluent) carried away by sewers. *Sewerage* refers to a system of sewers or a drainage system.
so	*So* is awkwardly ineffective as a conjunction and therefore should be avoided when possible.
soluble, solvable	*Soluble* means susceptible to being dissolved. Example: The material is *soluble* in alcohol. *Solvable* means susceptible to being resolved or explained. Example: The problem was not as *solvable* as anticipated.
some, somewhat	The adjective *some* should not be used for the adverb *somewhat*. Example: The method of duplication is *somewhat* (not *some*) less expensive.
stationary, stationery	*Stationary* means standing still. *Stationery* refers to writing materials.
verbal, oral	*Verbal* means written or spoken words. *Oral* means spoken.
vertex, vortex	*Vertex* refers to the intersection point of lines.

Vortex refers to the center of a fluid that is in a circular or whirling motion.

waive, wave   *Waive* means to relinquish, or to permit to pass.

Wave means to float in an air current, to motion with the hands, or a moving swell on the surface of a liquid.

while, though, and   *While* should only be used to express time relationships. It should not be used for *though* or *and*.

EXERCISES

1. What should be the general purposes of a report writing style?
2. Should a report writer define the following words in a report for aeronautical engineers: force, antenna, descent?
3. Why is cost-consciousness important in report writing?
4. Name three of the commonly found differences in readership that a report writer must consider before he begins to write.
5. Why should it be necessary to define the term *torque* and not define the term *engine* in a report to nontechnical readers?
6. What six questions must be answered to ensure thoroughness in a report?
7. What are words which symbolize things that can be detected by five senses called?
8. How should the report writer avoid the over-use of definitions?
9. Why has report writing become a more streamlined style of composition?

8

10. Write sentences correctly using the following:

a number	for	discover
the number	as	invent
many	fluid	capacity
much	liquid	ability

11. Write a criticism of a maintenance instruction manual for an item that has been purchased, such as an automobile or piece of shop equipment.

12. Define the following terms:

force	gasoline	envelop
energy	percent	envelope
work	percentage	mass
descent	mean	weight
dissent	median	maximum
ensure	mode	optimum
insure	due to	continual
gas	because of	continuous

13. Write a step-by-step procedure that tells a small child how to tie a bow knot in a shoe lace.

14. Write a procedure telling a man how to tie a bow knot behind his back when he puts on a carpenter's apron. (Hint: make it short.)

15. Which of the following abbreviations is most nearly correct? (One in each horizontal line.)

No.	No	no	no.
lb.	lb	lbs.	lbs
Gal.	gal.	Gal	Gals
10° F.	10 degF	10 deg.F	10°F
in	in.	″	In
ft.	ft	′	Ft
Hz	hz	hz.	Hz.
Sec	Sec.	sec	sec.
etc	etc.	ETC.	ETC

16. What do these abbreviations mean? (Look them up in a dictionary if you don't recognize them.)

sec	Hz	blk	Dec
msec	i.e.	pg	f.o.b.
lb	CI	constr.	fps
No.	AC	e.g.	pH
"	kcal	corp	a.m.
'	Btu	cu in.	etc.
°	B/L	cm	

17. Write abbreviations for these terms:

ounce	Hertz	technical
fluid ounce	week	New York
10 feet	volt	blue print
20 inches	ampere	3 yards
New Mexico	page	hour
Northwest	parts per million	calorie
1.5 ounces	3 quarts	watt
	September	

18. Rewrite those numbers that are wrong or that could be more properly written in another way:

one inch long	1/sixteenth in. bit
6.3×10^{-2}	0.02 in.
3.5 KCal	14x16x32″ high
.000063 in.	32.1 sec.
13,600,000,000 miles	14.2 M sec.
.025 cm	6,000 V

19. Write a report explaining your last trip from school to home. Include the *who, what, when, where, why,* and *how* of the situation. Write this report to an audience of adults who do not know you. These readers will determine if your means of transportation is effective; it is your function to give them the necessary facts to draw a conclusion.

20. Write an estimate report which shows the cost of operating your automobile on a *per mile basis*. (Include such costs as depreciation, insurance, etc.)

This man will be required to write a procedure for teaching other welders at his company how to operate this equipment safely. (Paul Lawrence Dunbar Vocational Highschool, Chicago, Illinois)

CHAPTER 5

Descriptions and Instructions

What is this object?

> It consists of a round metal shaft partially imbedded in a plastic handle. The handle has grooves to facilitate gripping by a human hand. The exposed part of the shaft has been flattened and beveled at the tip to form a thin, square edge. (44 words)

Most of us will say it's a screwdriver. But this object could just as well be a punch, a spatula, a chisel, or some other tool. Thus, the foregoing example illustrates a common problem in writing technique. How do you describe something in writing?

Since everyone knows what a screwdriver is, why couldn't we just say it's *a medium-sized slot screwdriver*. (5 words) We could—if we were giving instructions to an electronics technician. But what if the purpose of our description was to provide specifications to a company for manufacture of the screwdriver? Certainly, we would need much more detailed information such as the type of plastic in the handle, size of the shaft (length and diameter), type of steel in the shaft, etc. That's why it's so important to establish a purpose for your writing. Then, decide what the reader needs to know and give him the facts as precisely as you know how.

Describing an Object

Objects may be large, small, simple or complex, man-made or natural, but the technique of good description can be applied to all situations. This technique consists of three elements: an

71

introductory over-all description, a description of individual parts, and summary statements.

The introduction names the object, tells its purpose (if applicable), and lists individual parts. The individual parts description details physical characteristics about those parts. This information will include such factors as size, shape, color, material of construction, texture, finish, hardness, and relationship to other parts. Often, drawings or photographs are essential for presenting a useful description. (See Chapter 9.)

The summary tells how the over-all object works, where it may be found, how it is used, or other significant facts about it. Conclusions can be stated.

The following outline indicates the most effective approach to describing a device or an object:

With these concepts in mind, we can redescribe the screwdriver. Remember that all parts of the suggested outline (above) may not apply to every given case.

THE SCREWDRIVER

I. Introduction

This medium-sized slot-type screwdriver is a hand tool used to insert screws that fasten two pieces of construction material together. The unit is 8″ long and consists of two parts: a 6″ steel shaft and a 4″ plastic handle.

II. Individual Parts Description

A. Shaft

Separately, the round steel shaft is 6″ long, with a ¼″ diameter. It appears to be a particularly hard steel and has a chrome or zinc polished finish. Its function is to engage the screw slot and transfer energy from the handle (which is turned by the human hand) to drive screws.

On one end, 1½″ of the shaft has been flattened to a maximum width of ⅜″ and is tapered to a diamond shape, with a ¼″ wide square tip. This end is also beveled from two other sides to form the thin square tip, ³⁄₆₄″ thick.

The other end of the shaft has 1½″ of circular grooving machined ⅛″ apart. The grooved part of the shaft is imbedded 2″ deep in the end of a transparent plastic cylinder which serves as a handle. The machined grooves help prevent the shaft from working loose when pressures are applied to this tool.

B. Handle

The handle is a transparent plastic cylinder 4″ long, 1″ diameter. Six ¼″ wide grooves have been cast leng on the handle to facilitate gripping by the human hand. ~~Both~~ ends of the handle have been rounded off to prevent skin injuries when the handle is hand twisted. The handle transfers mechanical energy from the human hand to the shaft.

III. <u>Summary</u>

This medium-sized screwdriver is used to insert slot type screws of the No. 4 to 8 size range into predrilled holes. The eventual goal of inserting these screws is to fasten two pieces of construction material together, such as wood, plastic, or metal. The screws are driven through one piece of material and penetrate a second piece, cutting spiral grooves as they are driven inward. Tightening of this spiral groove occurs when the oversized head of the screw comes in contact with the surface material and thus mechanical tension holds the two pieces of construction material together. The screwdriver provides the user with a mechanical advantage which permits his hand to perform work it could not otherwise do.

Is the above description adequate? It doesn't tell the type of plastic from which the handle is made. It gives no specifications on the type of steel in the shaft, etc. So when does the writer quit writing his description? When good judgment tells him he has enough facts to accomplish his goal. Again, the screwdriver description given here does not contain enough data to permit manufacture of the tool. And it contains some superfluous sentences not required for manufacturing purposes. But it does serve as a good example in this book, and that's the purpose of it.

Describing a Process

A process is something that happens when a mechanism or device is used. A process also occurs in nature during life cycles. A process occurs when business transactions take place. In processes, material is moved, thoughts are developed, events happen—most importantly, energy is exchanged.

To describe a process, it is often important to know something about the components of that process. This may involve giving a physical description of a device prior to explaining how it works, or describing conditions prior to an event.

In describing a process which involves a mechanical device this outline is often sufficient:

I. Introduction
II. Required equipment and materials
III. Description of action steps
IV. Summary of expected or actual results

The *introduction* (Section I) tells the reader about the process in general terms. It tells *what* the process is and *why* it was performed. If applicable, the introduction may also tell *who* performs the process or *why* the process is being described.

Section II lists and describes any equipment or materials used to perform the processes. Section III discusses the individual steps (in proper sequence) that were accomplished to complete the process. Section IV gives a summary of expected or actual results.

With the suggested outline, let's describe the process of using a screwdriver to insert a screw:

PROPER TECHNIQUE FOR INSERTING A WOOD SCREW

I. Introduction

In this process, a medium-sized screwdriver was used as the main tool to fasten two pieces of ¾″ finished walnut wood together with one screw. Purpose of the demonstration was to show the proper technique for inserting a slot-type wood screw with a countersink head.

II. Equipment and materials

A. Equipment
1. (1) Electric drill (w/¼″ chuck)
2. (1) ⅛″ high-speed bit
3. (1) Countersink bit for No. 8 screw
4. (1) Medium-sized screwdriver
5. (1) Medium-sized table vise, mounted on bench

6. (1) Soft rag (preferably made from terry cloth or some other thick material)
7. (1) Lead marking pencil
8. (1) Retractable tape measure
9. (1) Felt tip pen w/red ink

B. Materials
1. (1) 1¼", No. 8 zinc-coated steel wood screw
2. (2) 1" × 2" × 12" pieces of finished walnut wood

III. Events

These steps were completed by the demonstrator:
1. The two pieces of walnut wood were placed together with the 2" sides facing one another.
2. The two pieces of walnut were then wrapped with the terry cloth; one 3" end of the wood pieces was left protruding from the cloth wrapping.
3. The wrapped wood pieces were placed horizontally in the vise with the ¾" edges up. Then, the jaws were tightened on that portion of the wood wrapped by cloth. This prevented the vice jaws from scarring or denting the wood. The 3" exposed wood ends were left protruding from the right side of the vise jaws. Prior to final tightening of the jaws, the wood pieces were adjusted to be perfectly aligned with one another.
4. The demonstrator then measured a position on the exposed wood ends, where he planned to insert the screw, and marked the spot with a point—using the lead pencil. This point was located 1½" from the end of the boards and was centered on the 2" face side.
5. Using the felt tip pen, the ⅛" high-speed bit was marked at a point 1¼" from the tip.
6. The bit was fastened in the electric drill chuck and a horizontal pilot hole (1¼" deep) was drilled into the wood pieces at the point described and marked under Item 4. The demonstrator used his red mark on the high-speed bit to indicate when drilling depth should be stopped.
7. The countersink bit was then placed in the electric drill and a cone-shaped cut was drilled into the ⅛" hole. This cone was slightly smaller than the countersink head on the steel screw.
8. The screw was then placed into the hole and pressed by hand until it would stay in place without support.
9. The screwdriver was inserted in the screw slot. Using the left-hand fingers to steady the screw, the screwdriver was turned clockwise by the demonstrator's right hand. The demonstrator applied sufficient pressure to the screw, as he was turning it, to drive it horizontally into the two pieces of

wood. He stopped turning when the screw head was tightly embedded in the hole, flush with the wood surface.

10. The attached wood pieces were then removed from the vise.

IV. Results

The screw did hold the two pieces of wood firmly together, but since only one screw was used the pieces will tend to rotate around the point where the screw is located. To correct this problem, it would be necessary to use two (or more) screws to fasten the wood pieces together. The demonstration did show the proper technique for inserting a wood screw.

Other Descriptions

Previously, we have described a process in which equipment and materials were used. But what about descriptions of events or conditions such as an industrial accident, a production line failure, or new quality control measures? These kinds of descriptions can be made in much the same manner as discussed above. Descriptions should always contain: (1) an *introduction* —which tells the reader about the circumstances in general terms; (2) a sequential *listing* or *discussion* of events and conditions; and (3) a *summary* of expected or actual results.

Instructions

To this point, we have discussed descriptions of objects and events in an impersonal way, simply telling how conditions were or what happened. Often the communicator must tell someone else how to do something. This form of writing is an instruction calling for action to take place in the present in a precise way. This means that instead of writing:

> The screw was then driven into the pilot hole with a clockwise turning motion.

. . . You should talk directly to the reader. Don't be afraid to use the word *you*.

> *Drive* the screw into the pilot hole with a clockwise turning motion. By using this technique, *you* will find . . .

Usually, the same outline applied to describing a process can also be applied to giving instructions where equipment and materials are involved:

I. Introduction

II. Required equipment and materials

III. Action steps

IV. Expected or actual results

Specifications

Specifications are a special kind of instruction but, instead of telling the reader *how* something is done, specs usually tell *what* the expected results should be. Writing is active with emphasis on the future. The verbs *will be* and *shall be* are often used.

Consider this specification for electrical work to be accomplished in new house construction:

ELECTRICAL WORK

A. General

    All electrical equipment (including wiring) shall be installed in accordance with the attached architectural drawings and will conform to city building codes. All materials shall be new and conform to standards of Underwriter's Laboratories, Inc.

B. Service

    Size of electric service shall be 125 amps, with 1/0 gage lines brought in from a point designated by the Utility Company. A main disconnect switch will be provided in a steel cabinet. This cabinet will also contain a breaker switch for each circuit.

C. Circuits

    Branch circuits will be No. 12 gage copper wire. Connections shall not be taped but will be covered with screw caps. Appliance circuits will be copper wire in the following sizes: (1) range, No. 8, 3-wire; (2) furnace and air conditioner, No. 12, 2-wire; (3) dryer, No. 10, 3-wire; (4) dishwasher, No. 12, 2-wire; (5)

garbage disposer, No. 12, 2-wire; (6) small motor, No. 12, 2-wire; (7) electric water heater, No. 12, 3-wire; (8) door bell, No. 18 wire.

D. Switches, receptacles and plates

All switches and double-wall receptacles will be installed according to the attached architectural drawings. Switches will be the silent type. All connection boxes will be metal; plates will be white plastic, and when switches are grouped, gang plates will be installed.

E. Special items

Special outlets will be installed according to the architectural plan for: 2 clocks, attic ventilating fans, thermostats and heating-cooling controls, television jacks, and stereophonic sound speaker extensions, overhead automatic garage door openers, and eave-mounted floodlights.

Obviously, this is not a specification written for use by a do-it-yourself weekend specialist. He would find relatively little value here. But a journeyman electrician would have no trouble installing this job—provided he had the architectural drawings.

Writing Approaches

As previously said many times in this book, there is no one best way to write on any subject. Your approach must consider the audience and its needs. When you are required to convey technical information in writing, select an outline (see Chapter 7) and start putting the words down on paper. Keep rewriting until you're satisfied. If you are writing instructions or specifications, always test them under actual working conditions to ensure that their completeness and validity will achieve the expected result.

EXERCISES

1. Examine these photographs and write 100-word descriptions of what is taking place in any two of them.

2. Describe *two* of these items:
   a. Carpenter's hammer
   b. Sheet metal or wood screw
   c. Paper clip
   d. Epoxy glue
   e. Coaxial cable
   f. Human red blood cell
   g. A rock
   h. Safety pin
   i. Elastic band (rubber)
   j. Yoke on TV set
   k. Lead pencil
   l. Slide rule

3. Describe *one* of the following:
   a. Chicken egg
   b. Egg beater
   c. Brace and bit
   d. Soldering gun
   e. Electrical resistor
   f. Paramecium
   g. Small butane torch
   h. Printed circuit board
   i. Welding rod
   j. Heat sink
   k. Kitchen sink
   l. Circuit breaker
   m. Thermostat
   n. Torque wrench

4. Describe *one* of these complex mechanisms:
   a. 1965 Ford Mustang
   b. 1935 Ford sedan
   c. Internal combustion engine
   d. Television set
   e. Human heart
   f. Building elevator system
   g. Four-burner electric cook top
   h. Four-burner natural gas cook top
   i. Refrigerator
   j. Air conditioning unit
   k. Self-venting toilet
   l. Surveyor's transit
   m. Bicycle

5. Describe *two* of these processes:
   a. How a bank checking account works
   b. Human kidney function
   c. Operation of internal combustion engine
   d. Photosynthesis
   e. Use of an ammeter
   f. Use of an oscilloscope
   g. Mixing red mortar for brick laying
   h. Sawing brick with a brick saw
   i. Electrical storm front
   j. Framing a house wall (2″×4″ construction)
   k. Painting a door jamb
   l. Operating a typewriter
   m. Using $a^2 + b^2 = c^2$
   n. Electrowinning
   o. Chrome plating of steel
   p. Steel open-hearth
   q. Copper ore smelting

6. Your instructor will perform a process in class such as sawing a board in half, soldering a wire connection, or exploding a toy balloon. Write a description of that process.
7. Rewrite the process your instructor performed in class as instructions telling someone how to do it.
8. Review an instruction manual from a small electric appliance or tool—an electric drill, an automatic toaster, a portable power saw, or a kitchen blender. Write a critical review of the manner in which operating instructions are given.
9. Write instructions telling someone how to operate an automobile with a three-speed manual shift transmission. Assume that this person knows about cars, and has ridden in them, but does not know how to drive.
10. Describe how an electric motor converts electrical energy into mechanical energy.

The employee shown here is responsible for continuous inspection of these hydraulic cylinders during manufacture. He collects data on each manufactured lot. Then he writes periodic reports on any irregularity of parts, or failure to meet quality control standards, which would result in the production of a defective product. (Bruning Co.)

CHAPTER 6

Gathering Facts and Sorting Data

As noted in Chapter 4, truth is the foremost quality of a report. Obviously, this truth depends first upon the writer's thoroughness in gathering facts for the report. There is no actual report without facts. Opinions, ideas, and decisions are derived from facts.

One trait that a report writer needs is a respect for facts. Too often, facts are not made the basis for important decisions because someone has failed to take the time to gather the material. It is then that opinions become the basis upon which decisions are made. The report writer's job is to produce a document which will form the basis for an intelligent decision. If the facts are wrong, or incomplete, then a correct decision can be made only by accident. It is facts that permit people in business, industry, and government to do their jobs and do them efficiently.

Gathering facts, perhaps, is the most difficult but also the most important part of report writing. The process requires considerable time and effort. Regardless of whether the report is long or short, formal or informal, there are a number of facts that the investigator must know before preparing a report on a subject. Prior to obtaining their facts many professional report writers prepare a preliminary outline with main headings and as many subheadings as possible, covering the intended scope of the subject. (See Chapter 7.) This permits the writer to conduct his investigation in a more fruitful and efficient manner—saving time for both the writer and the people being interviewed.

Gathering facts involves many different kinds of activity. The activity varies with the type of problem and the type of report. These facts, the general sources from which facts can be obtained, and the analysis of data are the subjects of this chapter. Note-taking, a necessity for the accuracy required in report writing, is also examined.

Definition of Facts

Facts mean the basic information from which the writer constructs a report. Many such facts can eventually be counted, measured, or expressed mathematically. This objective information is thus in contrast with the opinions that the writer uses in parts of the report such as the introduction, summary, conclusions, and recommendations. However, if the writer does the job properly, these opinions will reflect the numerical information contained in the body of the report. Therefore, even opinions are linked closely to verifiable facts in report writing.

General Sources of Facts

Just how a writer finds the material depends upon the subject of the report. If the subject is one with which the writer is familiar, personal knowledge can be used. Unfortunately, the report writer is seldom in a position to just write a report from such personal knowledge without obtaining more facts. This knowledge is useful to the writer, of course. It serves as a foundation from which the report can be written. From this knowledge the writer often knows where to begin and which questions to ask first. Gathering facts, or at least more facts, usually is an unavoidable task in writing a complete and meaningful report.

The successful report writer gathers material with objectivity and precision—distinguishing between the important and the trivial. It is important to be thorough. It is embarrassing to return and ask for additional information. It is the report writer's responsibility to seek the most accurate, up-to-date and complete sources of facts.

Observing. In writing many types of reports, personal observation is essential. In this method of gathering material, the writer is able to see his subject and record the findings and observations. The exact information that is needed can be obtained without depending upon someone else to remember and relate the details.

In most situations, recording information while making the observation is an excellent idea. Recording the information usually involves not only taking notes but measuring and making sketches of objects. A writer making such observations often has such equipment as notebooks, questionnaires, sketch pads, and measuring devices. Measuring devices could be simple items such as a tape measure or a thermometer—or a complex device such as an oscilloscope.

Sampling. A large percentage of the conclusions found in reports, especially examination reports, are based upon the process known as sampling. The principle of sampling involves testing a representative part which is assumed to be representative of the whole lot of parts.

With a homogeneous product, such as a metal rod or a strand of electrical wire, which has been produced in large quantity lots, a test of a small piece taken from any of the finished product will serve as a test of the lot. Consequently, sampling products such as metals, coal, oil, cement, and soil is a rather simple process. The proper methods have been established by those specialists in each field of work.

The sampling of a mixed or heterogeneous group, such as people, however, is a different problem. A larger sample is required, and often special methods must be used to ensure reliability. For example, the person preparing a report on what the people of an area prefer as the route for a prospective highway between two cities, must first decide how to select a sample of these citizens for questioning. The vocational writer, following modern practice, will try to make the sample representative by making certain that each significant element of the citizenry is included in the right proportions. This might include a portion of people from each county and town, a portion from each general occupation (industrial workers, farmers, business people, professionals) and a portion of both vehicle owners and non-vehicle owners. It can thus be seen that sampling from a heterogeneous group can be complex.

Interviewing. The interview is an important and effective method of securing facts. Interviews with persons well informed on the subject often eliminate the need for extensive personal study. A writer faced with preparing a progress report on a pipeline construction project may find that the only logical method of finding out what is causing the delay in the completion of the project is to talk to the welders, pipefitters, and other craftsmen working on the job.

The best interviewer, of course, is the one who can obtain the necessary information in the shortest time and with the least amount of friction between people. This means that the interview must be planned. Before beginning an interview, the report writer should:

    (1) Know exactly what is to be discussed, keeping in mind the aim and purpose of the report

    (2) Know what raw data must be obtained

    (3) Have some specific questions prepared

The report writer must ask useful questions. At the same time, the interview should be more than merely a question-and-answer session. The highly-trained interviewer learns quickly the type of question that will elicit the desired information and will also leave the person at ease. Many people dislike being asked questions in rapid order and prefer to tell a story. Often such persons talk away from the subject and must be drawn back diplomatically through the use of appropriate questions.

To be sure of retaining all the information gathered, various types of recording devices are used by interviewers today. This practice depends upon the availability of such devices and whether the person being interviewed consents to the use of it. A tape recorder is a valuable piece of equipment when one is trying to ensure accuracy and completeness, as the report writer must.

If a recording device is not used, the interviewer must depend upon memory, or take notes. It is often impossible to remember all of the facts gathered during an interview. Note-taking then becomes essential. The interviewer must listen carefully, fixing in mind the more important statements.

If notes are not taken during the interview, a brief write-up of the meeting should be prepared while it is fresh in the interviewer's mind.

Reading. The nature of some reports does not require the writer to search for facts other than those that have already been published. In preparing such reports, the writer's aim may be to:

(1) Use a different approach than that used by previous writers

(2) Use more up-to-date material than written in previous documents

(3) Make greater evaluation of data already compiled

The success of such a report still depends upon how well informed the writer is upon the subject. Only in this case, gathering the facts is confined to reading material.

In some cases the writer may need to do some background reading on the subject to fill in details or to add facts which were not found elsewhere.

The reading may be limited entirely to the files of the writer's own company or organization. Documents such as contracts, catalogs, brochures, manufacturers' publications, published and unpublished reports, records, specifications, and drawings are often kept just for such a purpose.

The writer may find the published reports of federal, state, county, and municipal agencies in libraries. Libraries may also have such material as experiment station bulletins, reports published by universities and privately endowed foundations, and sometimes, reports published by individuals.

A report writer should become familiar with the library *indexes* that can provide sources of material for given subjects. *The Engineering Index* is a frequently used index to science and engineering subjects. The writer conducting a literature search may check *The Engineering Index* for previous articles or major reports on a subject. *The Applied Science and Technology Index* and the *Business Periodicals Index* are also valuable to the report writer. Specialized indexes are also published in the various fields of science and engineering.

Abstracts generally present more complete summaries of particular articles than do indexes. There are several abstracting services that publish abstracts for particular science and engineering fields.

The report writer trying to gather current material on a given subject is generally more successful using indexes and abstracts than books. Because of time lags in writing, publishing, and cataloging, technical books are at least several months out of date when they become available to the researcher. Therefore, it is a mistake to check only the library card catalog which only lists books on various subjects. Articles often appear before the first book is available on a technical subject.

The source of the material should be clearly indicated in the report. People who have written books and technical papers deserve to have credit for the information used.

Questionnaire. The report writer should not rely upon a questionnaire when other means of obtaining facts are available. Even under the most favorable circumstances, only a small percentage of replies, often ten to twenty percent, can be expected from those to whom the questionnaire is addressed. Yet, it is obviously necessary in many investigations.

The writer is asking a favor whenever requesting that a questionnaire be completed. Usually, there are no sales possibilities involved with the inquiry. The writer is only seeking information. The task is to prepare the questionnaire in such a way as to produce the maximum number of answers and make it simple and clear enough so that the answers are usable when received. Note these few rules when preparing a questionnaire:

(1) Make the inquiry friendly and respectful.

(2) Include only those questions that are essential.

(3) Ask simple and clear questions.

(4) Test each question for clarity—make sure there is only one possible interpretation.

(5) Prepare questions that do not require too much time or trouble for the person completing the questionnaire: Is the catalyst used in all laboratory experiments?
    Yes ( )   No ( )
If not, in what percentage of experiments is the catalyst generally used:
    1 to 25% ( )   26 to 50% ( )
    51 to 75% ( )   76 to 100% ( )

(6) Do not use questions that suggest the answer:
    Poor: Did you oppose the inadequate design at the beginning of the project?
    Better: Did you agree ( ) or disagree ( ) with the design at the beginning of the project?

(7) Generally avoid questions that call for an opinion. It is usually facts that the report writer is seeking. If an opinion is needed, make it understood that it is an opinion that is desired.

Usually a questionnaire is accompanied by a short, tactful letter. The letter is used to make a courteous request for help. The writer should briefly explain the purpose of the investigation and why information is being sought from the reader. A brief statement of praise, avoiding flattery, should be used if the reader is a recognized authority upon the subject. Any possible benefit for the reader should be emphasized. The assistance and cooperation of the reader should be urged in the closing of the letter. A stamped, return addressed envelope should accompany the letter and questionnaire.

Study the following:

                                        Allen-Jones Steel Company
                                        Salt Lake City, Utah 84070
                                        March 20, 19--

ARC Chemical Company
Post Office Box 42
Salt Lake City, Utah 84112

Attention: Mr. R. M. Milibrew,
             Chief Engineer

Dear Mr. Milibrew:

   As a manufacturing foreman with Allen-Jones Steel Company, I am preparing a report upon the extreme conditions to which our various grades of two-inch pipe are subjected, especially in chemical plants.

   Knowing that you conducted extensive resarch before deciding to use Allen-Jones pipe and that it has been in use at your plant for two years now, I am writing to you in the hope that you will complete the questionnaire and return it to me in the enclosed envelope.

   If a copy of our finished report would be of use to you, please indicate this on the questionnaire and a copy will be forwarded to you.

   I believe that your authoritative answers to the questions are essential to ensure a complete, factual report. Any additional information that you may see fit to include will be very much appreciated.

                                        Very truly yours,

                                        W. C. Boyd
                                        Manufacturing Foreman

WCB/mw
Enc: As stated.

Taking Notes

The report writer learns early that a systematic and consistent means of recording information must be used. Even those writers with good memories should not rely on memory alone. It is often essential to keep original records after they have been used in preparing the report. Such records may be used in making patent applications, in legal proceedings, or simply for future reference. With these thoughts in mind, the writer should be prepared to record the information in permanent form.

Just how extensive and careful the report writer should be in taking notes generally depends upon:

(1) The type of information that must be gathered

(2) The other purposes for which the recorded information might be used

(3) How much information must be gathered

(4) The requirements of the writer's employer

(5) Whether sources must be quoted exactly

(6) Costs and time involved

Regardless of the situation surrounding the note taking, the writer must be sure that: (1) the facts will be clearly understandable in the future, and (2) the facts can be used effectively in writing the report.

Prior to beginning the actual note taking, the writer should draw up a preliminary outline. At this stage, this outline may or may not resemble the final one used to arrange the material in the report. This outline will serve as a crude system for classifying the facts as they are obtained. A simple outline for the report on the extreme conditions to which various grades of two-inch pipe are subjected might be divided into sections as shown.

Preliminary Outline
TWO-INCH GRADE YZ PIPE USAGE

1. Analysis of pipe used prior to the availability of the new types and grades
2. Development of the new types and grades
3. Research on pipe usage with various chemicals and solutions
   a. Heat resistance
   b. Corrosion resistance
   c. Acid resistance
4. Other uses
5. Miscellaneous information

Again, such an outline is crude and there may be overlapping, as in corrosion and acid resistance, but it does provide a basis for dividing a mass of facts into categories. It also gives the writer an idea of what facts must be recorded during the note taking.

There are various materials used successfully by report writers in taking notes. Those commonly used include:

(1) Legal pads
(2) Notebooks
(3) Index cards
(4) Punched cards
(5) Laboratory notebooks
(6) Preprinted forms
(7) Commercially-produced forms

The advantages and disadvantages of each should be reviewed before choosing the best one for a particular assignment.

There are three general but useful rules that a writer should remember before taking the first note:

(1) *Take enough notes.* When the writer has found answers to the questions, all the facts needed from that source should be recorded. Remember that the report will have to be written from the notes.

(2) *Take only the necessary notes.* There is no point in taking notes that do not answer the questions about the subject. This rule is easily followed if the preparatory work has been done by the writer.

(3) *Record the source of the facts.* Whether the facts come from an interview, a personal observation or from a printed source, following this rule will often save the writer time and trouble. The date and location of the observation should be part of the notes. For interviews, the name and title of the person interviewed, and the location and date should be recorded. If the material is taken from a printed source, the author, title, publication date and page number should be noted.

Analyzing Data[1]

In addition to facts, a report offers statements of problems and opinions based on facts, states methods used in obtaining the facts, answers questions, and may give conclusions and instructions. A report is far more than some pages of raw data. These data, after being gathered, must be analyzed and organized in a manner that will be meaningful to the reader. This, again, is the job of the report writer. For example, placing the legend "Table I" alone in text has little significance to the reader even though the contents of the table may be excellent. The table lacks the necessary textual explanation required to make the data meaningful.

Examine the following table and its textual reference. Table I presents an example of raw data gathered on equipment times (hours) until failure.

The data in Table I obviously fail to answer the following questions:

(1) What is the problem?

---

[1] For additional information on table and graph preparation, see Chapter 9.

TABLE I.	EQUIPMENT TIMES UNTIL FAILURE (Seven-month period in hours)					
June	July	Aug	Sept	Oct	Nov	Dec
400	1050	1100	1050	1500	1200	890
1300	1200	1410	600	1050	1350	850
500	1750	2150	1100	900	1700	1400
1100	1300	800	1400	1200	150	1500
800	700	950	1650	1000	1100	750

(2) Under what conditions were the data gathered?

(3) Why are these data cited?

(4) What is the reliability of the data?

(5) What conclusions can be drawn from these data?

Until the writer answers these, and other important questions, the information in the table, regardless of how factual, is meaningless. The task for the writer is to analyze the data and change them from meaningless to meaningful facts. A good text description of the data is:

> The values shown in Table I represent the time until failure of a piece of equipment (name it) during a seven-month period.

To provide a meaningful presentation, the writer must analyze the data; but analyzing large amounts of unorganized data becomes cumbersome. Therefore, the writer usually groups the data in some convenient way. The data in Table I, for example, could be examined more effectively by grouping the values (called observations) as shown in Table II. The data have been divided into intervals of equal size, and the number of failures which fall into each interval have been tallied. The values shown in the fourth column are called *absolute frequencies*. The fifth column contains the tally of the number of failures and is called the *absolute cumulative frequency*. The entire table, which shows the distribution of the values, is known as an *absolute frequency distribution*.

In Fig. 1, a bar graph is used to make the data even clearer. The dashed line is an almost symmetrical bell-shaped curve. It is centered around the 900 to 1149 hour limits.

No.	Class Interval Limits (Hours)		Tally	Absolute Frequency	Absolute Cumulative Frequency
	(1)	(2)	(3)	(4)	(5)
–	From	To			
1	150	– 399	1	1	1
2	400	– 649	111	3	4
3	650	– 899	11111 1	6	10
4	900	– 1149	11111 11111	10	20
5	1150	– 1399	11111 1	6	26
6	1400	– 1649	11111	5	31
7	1650	– 1899	111	3	34
8	1900	– 2150	1	1	35

Table II.   ANALYSIS OF OPERATING TIMES UNTIL FAILURE (MILL NO. 7)

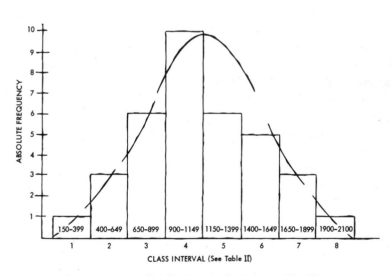

Fig. 1. Frequency distribution graph of No. 7 mill failures.

With the data now arranged in a table and graph, the writer may proceed to analyze and explain the information that has been gathered. Certain measures are used to describe the data. Some of these measures characterize the central body of the data. Frequently, the mean or average, the median, and the mode are employed for this purpose.

The *mean* is simply the sum of all the values, or observations, divided by the total number of values. In our example the mean is:

$$\frac{\text{(Taken from Table I) } 400 + 1300 + 500 + \ldots + 750}{\text{(Taken from Table II) } 35} = 1110$$

The *median* is the middle value of the data, or the point at which half the values are the same as or greater and half are the same as or smaller than it. The median in Table I is 1100. (Write the numbers out to prove it.)

The *mode* is the value that occurs most often or the value around which the other values tend to concentrate. In Table I, the mode is also 1100. If the distribution is perfectly symmetrical, the mean, median and mode will all be the same value.

After the central tendency of the data is known, often it is desirable to know the degree to which the values tend to spread away from the central value or how the data are distributed within the extreme limits. This is called the *dispersion* of the data. Three of the more common measures of dispersion are range, variance, and standard deviation.

The *range* is the difference between the upper and lower limits. The range in Table I is 2000 hours (2150 to 150 hrs).

The *variance* is the sum of the squares of the *differences* between the values and the mean value, all divided by the total number of values. The variance in Table I is:

$$(400 - 1110)^2 + \ldots + (750 - 1110)^2 = 154{,}270$$

The *standard deviation* is simply the square root of the variance. The standard deviation in our example is approximately 392 hours.

Other factors such as trends, peaks, troughs, patterns, and

various mathematical relationships may need to be analyzed, depending upon the type and amount of data and the purpose of the report. It is beyond the scope of this book to discuss each of these factors. Adequate material is available to writers who need reference material upon statistical analysis.

After analyzing the data that has been gathered, the report writer, finally, must decide whether the data are significant. The data should substantiate, to the fullest possible extent, the conclusions that are to be drawn in the report. If the data fail to do this, the writer, depending upon limitations of time, budget, and resources, may need to gather and analyze more data.

There are times when a writer is unable to obtain more data for some reason. It is then the writer's duty to tell the readers about the limitations of data in the report. This will prevent readers from questioning the conclusions and wondering why the limitations of the data were not considered by the writer.

EXERCISES

1. What is the most important part of report writing?
2. Why is a report writer, who is trying to gather *current* material, generally more successful using indexes and abstracts rather than technical books alone?
3. What are the three general rules that a report writer should remember before taking the first note for an assignment? Explain why each rule is important.
4. Determine the *mode, mean,* and *median* of the following sets of numbers.

A	B	C	D	E	F	G
1	50	100	1.5	13	0.00003	6.2×10^{-1}
2	60	250	1.6	14	0.00016	6.3×10^{-1}
3	70	600	1.7	15	0.0023	4.4×10^{-3}
4	80	1000	1.9	16	0.00019	2.2×10^{-1}
5	90	300	3.4	17	0.0001	2.4×10^{-3}
		200	4.6	18	0.0006	6.6×10^{-4}
		50	2.7		0.0013	2.2×10^{-2}
			19.2		0.011	1.4×10^{-1}
			3.6		0.114	1.3×10^{-2}

5. Determine the *range, variance,* and *standard deviation* of columns A, B, C, D and E in Exercise 4.
6. At a construction site welders worked the following man-hours to complete the same repetitive task:

Man-Hours for Completing Task				
June	July	August	September	November
131	152	181	134	192
133	153	171	137	193
146	142	172	145	183
144	165	162	155	184
141	175	169	156	199
154	177	163	156	194
	160	166	152	182
	163	162	166	189
		161	169	179
			176	

a. Using these class interval limits, construct an analysis (similar to Table II, page 95) of man-hour times to complete this task:

    (1) 130-139   (3) 150-159   (5) 170-179   (7) 190-199
    (2) 140-149   (4) 160-169   (6) 180-189

b. Determine the *mode, mean, median* and *standard deviation* of these man-hours.
c. Grouped by the month, determine the *median hours* spent to do the task each month. What can you conclude from this summary?

7. Determine from your classmates how far each one travels to school each day. Record this data and, using the distance traveled as the class interval limits, prepare an absolute frequency distribution table and a frequency distribution bar graph. (See Chapter 9 in addition to information in this chapter.)
8. Determine the mean, median, and mode of the data obtained in Exercise 7.
9. Write a paragraph stating the limitations of data gathered in Exercise 7.
10. Define dispersion.

11. List six of the items that generally determine how extensive and detailed the report writer should be in taking notes.

12. Prepare a list of questions for an interview with one of the following:

    a. An engineer upon the advantages and disadvantages of his profession.

    b. A skilled workman upon his working conditions.

    c. A research scientist upon the purpose of his research.
       ... in completing this exercise, select a specific field such as electronics, carpentry, etc.

13. What is the principle upon which sampling is based?

14. Why is it often necessary to employ special methods when sampling heterogeneous subjects?

15. Gather and record the facts necessary to prepare a progress report upon a building (can be a home) under construction in the area. Consider each of these items as individual components of construction:

    a. Excavation
    b. Footings
    c. Foundation walls
    d. Framing
    e. Plumbing (rough)
    f. Plumbing (finish)
    g. Electrical wiring (rough)
    h. Electrical (finish)
    i. Heating and air conditioning
    j. Insulation
    k. Drywall
    l. Brick or siding
    m. Exterior soffit and fascia
    n. Chimney and fireplace
    o. Windows
    p. Finish carpentry (interior and exterior)
    q. Roofing
    r. Foundation backfill
    s. Cabinets and fixtures
    t. Painting and finish work
    u. Floor coverings

16. Prepare a questionnaire that you would use to obtain facts for the progress report required in Exercise 15.

17. Prepare a letter requesting that the questionnaire required in Exercise 16 be completed and returned.

Every disaster has a cause. The cause of this fire will be analyzed by the men who worked in the area. They will use the scientific method in conducting their investigation. They will write reports, based on their observation and knowledge. Use of the scientific method of reasoning will aid you in solving many vocational and vocational writing problems, if you will take time to use it. (Official U. S. Navy Photograph)

CHAPTER 7

Planning the Report

After the facts are gathered and analyzed, some writers think that they are ready to start putting sentences and paragraphs on paper. Most of the better vocational writers know, however, that the actual writing seldom begins at this point. Those who are anxious to charge headlong into the writing phase often find that their writing is unclear, or they just do not know how to continue what they have started. It is at this moment that the frustrated writer realizes that he has a beginning to a report that really is no beginning because it leads nowhere.

So, just to start writing is not the way to begin. Who would try to build a workbench or a bookshelf, for example, without some idea of the materials to be used, how the object is to be constructed, and how it will look when finished? As in any other task that requires considerable effort, a person should have a *plan* before beginning to write a report. The *outline* is that plan.

Organizing the Material

Organization of the report material should be the first thought that the writer gives to planning his document. The amount and complexity of the material to be presented determines not only the length, but also the makeup of the report in general.

Most vocational writers are in close agreement as to the general approach in organizing. This approach consists of stating the problem, describing what was done, discussing the results, and presenting the conclusions and recommendations. The approach is based on the scientific method of reasoning that has been so important in our Western culture. It is one of the most important concepts you will ever learn because, if applied effectively, you can use it to solve most of your vocational problems as well as writing problems.

The scientific method includes these six steps:

THE SCIENTIFIC METHOD

1. Problem exists
2. Obtain facts about problem
3. Study facts
4. Propose solution
5. Test solution
6. Formulate conclusion

You can see how the scientific method is applied to the elements of a report outline in the following illustration.

SCIENTIFIC METHOD

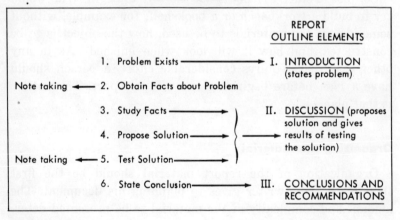

Although most people seem to think that this type of report organization is obvious and natural, it is not accepted by everyone who writes reports. Some writers give the results and conclusions near the beginning and describe in subsequent sections how they were obtained. Obvious advantages exist for both types of organization, but most readers and most writers appear to prefer the scientific method because it is based on a logical sequence of investigation.

Since the straightforward, scientific type of organization does follow normal logic and has long been accepted by both report writers and readers, it is recommended here. The reader who wants to see the results and conclusions first can turn to the back of the report. Thus, the logical sequence of the presentation remains intact.

Identifying the Objective and Main Ideas

Every writer has a definite purpose in mind when preparing a report. The purpose may be to show the progress on a particular project, to show the results of an experiment, or to justify the purchase of a piece of equipment. The writer should take the time to clarify the specific purpose in his mind. Keeping the purpose in mind helps the writer stay on the subject and reduces the chances of including unessential material.

After establishing the purpose, the writer should identify the main ideas needed to support the purpose and plan those ideas in the report.

Assuming that a writer's purpose is to justify the design and fabrication of a new piece of inspection equipment, answers to the following questions should provide the main ideas for the support of the objective:

(*What?*)   Design and fabricate new inspection equipment
(*Where?*) Quality Control Department
(*When?*)   By July 1, 19—
(*Who?*)   Plant engineering and machine shop
(*How?*)   Using existing materials and personnel
(*Why?*)   Inaccuracy of present equipment
(*Why?*)   Excessive inspection time

The emphasis is on the *why* questions. The answers to these two questions should be an important part of the presentation. All the answers represent the main ideas and should not be confused with the facts, figures, or examples that may be used to support them.

Outlining

Any report can be written more quickly and logically from an *outline,* whether it is a very simple outline or a very complicated one that is several pages long. A statement of objectives and main ideas can be easily expanded into a working outline. This is done by filling in the supporting ideas and adding the introduction, conclusions, and recommendations.

An outline, then, is a schematic statement of the material in a report, showing the order in which the material is presented and the relationship between the various topics. Once the outline is made, the writer can focus on one section of the report at a time. To aid him in this task, each section of the report should be put in a separate manila folder. The writing, thus, becomes easier. Since the outline shows where each point is to be made, the writer does not have to worry about this problem as he prepares the report. In other words, he can write with confidence.

An outline is perhaps more valuable in vocational writing than in any other type of writing. By using an outline as the framework upon which to create the report, a writer is often able to recognize missing pieces or poor organization. An outline not only saves the writer's time but it also saves the reader's time because it helps ensure a well-organized report which covers the subject.

Types of Outlines (Examples)

The type of outline that a writer should use depends upon:

(1) Whether the report is being prepared to conform to a required format
(2) Whether the reporting form must be approved before the report is submitted
(3) The experience of the writer in preparing the type of report
(4) The writer's knowledge of the subject
(5) The complexity, formality and length of the report

Some reports, such as those prepared under contracts, must conform to a set form. The basic sections of the outline are thus established for the writer of such reports.

If the outline must be approved before the report is submitted, a formal type of outline generally is expected.

Most report writers, however, have great latitude in selecting the type of outline for their reports. Consequently, the writer's experience, knowledge of the subject, and the complexity, formality and length of the report are usually the determining factors in selecting the type of outline.

The writer preparing a letter or other short-form report (See Chapter 10) may choose to work from casual notes, often called a *scratch outline*. The notes are usually jotted down without regard to form, but with complete attention to their meaning.

However, the *heading outline* is the most common type of formal outline used by vocational writers. The headings are noted in brief phrases or in single words and are numbered or lettered consistently according to their rank in the report.

Types of heading outlines include: (1) standard English; (2) numerical; and (3) position-and-weight. Examples of these outlines follow.

Standard English Outline

DOCUMENT TITLE
(no more than seven words)

I. Main section heading

   A. First order sidehead

      1. Second order sidehead

         a. Third order sidehead

           1) Fourth order sidehead

              a) Fifth order sidehead

Numerical Outline

DOCUMENT TITLE
(no more than seven words)

1.0 Main section heading

   1.1 First order sidehead

      1.1.1 Second order sidehead

         1.1.1.1 Third order sidehead

            1.1.1.1.1 Fourth order sidehead

               1.1.1.1.1.1 Fifth order sidehead

Position-and-Weight Outline

DOCUMENT TITLE
(no more than seven words)

Main section heading

   First order sidehead

      Second order sidehead   Run into text ...

Now, let's re-examine these outlines in an actual report situation.

Standard English Outline

DESIGN AND FABRICATION
OF
INSPECTION EQUIPMENT

I Introduction

   A. Objective
   B. Background information
   C. Limitations of data

II Discussion

   A. Inaccuracy of present equipment

      1. Customer complaints
      2. Measurement studies

   B. Excessive inspection time

      1. Man-hour studies
      2. Time and motion studies

   C. Proposed inspection equipment

      1. Advantages

         a. Improved accuracy
         b. Reduced inspection time

      2. Disadvantages

         a. Initial cost
         b. Risk of using unproven equipment

III Conclusions and recommendations

   A. Conclusions
   B. Recommendations

Numerical Outline

DESIGN AND FABRICATION
OF
INSPECTION EQUIPMENT

1.0 Introduction

    1.1 Statement of objective
    1.2 Background of information
    1.3 Limitations of data

2.0 Discussion

    2.1 Inaccuracy of present equipment

        2.1.1 Customer complaints
        2.1.2 Measurement studies

    2.2 Excessive inspection time

        2.2.1 Man-hour studies
        2.2.2 Time and motion studies

    2.3 Proposed inspection equipment

        2.3.1 Advantages

            2.3.1.1 Improved accuracy
            2.3.1.2 Reduced inspection time

        2.3.2 Disadvantages

            2.3.2.1 Initial costs
            2.3.2.2 Risk of using unproven equipment

3.0 Conclusions and recommendations

    3.1 Conclusions
    3.2 Recommendations

Position-and-Weight Outline

DESIGN AND FABRICATION
OF
INSPECTION EQUIPMENT

Introduction

    Objective
    Background information
    Limitations of data

Inaccuracy of present equipment

    Customer complaints

    Measurement studies

    Excessive inspection time

        Man-hour studies   These studies were ...
        Time and motion studies   It was estimated ...

Proposed inspection equipment

Conclusions and recommendations

The *sentence outline* differs from a heading outline only in that each heading and subheading is a complete sentence. The major advantage of the sentence outline is that it requires the person preparing it to think through his ideas thoroughly so that a complete statement can be made. It is a more detailed type of outline and requires more time to prepare. A sentence outline of the discussion section of a report might look like the one shown on pages 110 to 111.

DESIGN AND FABRICATION
OF
INSPECTION EQUIPMENT

I. The advantage of the proposed inspection equipment over the present equipment

   are the improvement in accuracy and the reduction in inspection time.

   A. The inaccuracy of the present equipment has been demonstrated by the in-

      crease in customer complaints and the results of the measurement studies.

      1. Customer complaints have risen 21 percent during the last three

          months.

      2. The measurement studies show that 32 percent of the measurements

          taken are inaccurate.

   B. The excessive inspection time has been demonstrated with man-hour studies

      and with time and motion studies.

      1. The man-hour studies show that more man-hours are expended with

          the use of the present equipment than with any other inspection

          equipment.

      2. Time and motion studies show that too much time is expended in

          handling the pieces being inspected.

   C. The proposed inspection equipment has two major advantages and two dis-

      advantages.

      1. The advantages are the improvement in accuracy, and the reduc-

          tion of inspection time

          a. The design studies show that the improvement in accuracy

              will be 30 percent

          b. The inspection time is expected to be reduced by 24

              percent.

---

2. The disadvantages of the proposed equipment are the initial cost and the risk of using unproven equipment.

    a. The initial cost for the design and fabrication is expected to be $8000.

    b. The equipment has not been subjected to mass-production conditions, and the reliability from this standpoint has thus far not been demonstrated.

The most important thing for the vocational writer to remember in selecting an outline is that the material should be presented in the most useful form. The outline that helps you most in doing this is the one that should be used. Each has advantages and disadvantages. Sometimes a heading outline and sentence outline are combined, with the sentences written under the headings.

EXERCISES

1. In your own words, what is the definition of an outline?
2. After reading the section on types of outlines, which outline form do you think is used most frequently by experienced vocational writers?
3. Why does a report writer prepare an outline *after* the facts have been gathered? Should he ever prepare an outline before the facts are gathered?
4. Why is it important for a writer to keep the purpose in mind when preparing the outline and the report itself?
5. What is the scientific method? List its elements.
6. What is the scientific type of report organization? Do you think this is the best form of organization for reports that would be written in your field of vocational study? Why?

7. Here are some complaints voiced by the owners of new homes.

   a. My floors creak and groan with every step I take on them. It's driving me crazy.

   b. Our toilet drain pipes are always becoming clogged.

   c. We don't have enough water pressure to water our lawn, but our neighbors seem to have sufficient pressure.

   d. There isn't enough light in our kitchen or bathrooms.

   e. Odors linger in our kitchen and bathrooms.

   f. Our hollow-core interior doors have all warped.

   g. Our concrete walks and driveways are cracking, and the surfaces sluff off.

   i. Our furnace will not heat the house adequately in the coldest part of the winter.

   j. Our hot water runs out too soon. We can't even fill a bathtub or wash clothes without running out of hot water.

   k. We have developed many cracks in our drywall joints.

   l. We have to wait a long time for the hot water to come from the water heater to the bathroom sink. Sometimes the tap will run cold water for more than a minute before it warms up.

   m. We've had several leaks in our copper piping.

   n. Our intercom system has never worked right. It hums, and sometimes individual speakers won't work.

   o. Every time our furnace and refrigerator motors turn on, the lights go dim.

   p. The plastic countertops in our kitchen have worked loose.

   q. The furnace air is cold in some of our rooms and very hot in others. We can't maintain a uniform temperature throughout the house.

   r. Pools of water stand on our semi-flat composition roof.

   s. Our fireplace will not draw properly, and sometimes smoke comes into the living room.

   t. The linoleum in our kitchen and bathroom came up.

   u. The slightest hand adjustment of the hot and cold

water controls on our shower make the spray either too hot or too cold.

v. Cracks have developed, and the grouting has fallen out of the joint between our bathtub and the tile above it.

w. We smell gas in our basement. We're not sure whether the odor is from the sewer drains in the floor or from the gas line to our furnace.

x. Our basement concrete walls have cracked, and water leaks in.

y. We cannot get the contractor to complete minor work still remaining to be done on our new house.

Take two of these problems and, using the scientific method (see outline on page 102), solve the problem by writing a short report which gives the construction techniques necessary to solve these problems. Visit actual construction and home sites to gather information, if you can. Get assistance from your vocational instructors. Of course you may not be able to test your proposed solution, but assume that your proposed solution to the problem proved satisfactory in actual testing.

8. List, and show an example of three types of heading outlines.

9. What is the major advantage of a sentence outline? Should a heading outline and a sentence outline ever be combined?

10. Assume that you are to prepare a comprehensive report upon the design, fabrication, and installation of a computer-operated lathe. What type of outline would you choose for this report? Why?

11. Prepare a heading outline showing the subject matter in a technical description of a ball-point pen. (Take the pen apart to examine the parts.)

12. The purpose is to justify the purchase of welding equipment costing $6000 for use in a production operation. The facts are:

Welding will reduce the present material cost by 10 percent and the production man hours by 15 percent.

Welding will improve the strength of the manufactured part by eight percent.

The present material cost is $62,000 a year.

The new welding equipment could be installed by September 15, 19—.

The welding equipment could be installed by the Engineering and Maintenance Department.

Welding would increase the inspection time of the finished parts by 12 percent.

There are no qualified welders among the Company's present employees.

Production employees are paid $4.50 an hour.

Welders would be paid $6.50 an hour.

From these facts, develop the main ideas for the support of the objective. After developing the main ideas, prepare a heading outline for a report on justification for the purchase of the welding equipment. Then, prepare a separate sentence outline for the report.

13. Write a combined heading and sentence outline for this report.

Testing Oil Additives and 10-20 Motor Oil for Effect in Reduction Friction Down a V-ramp.

I had seen television commercials on motor oil additives which left the viewer with the impression that these substances were very slick and would reduce friction greatly under any circumstances. I decided to test this fact for myself and write a report on it.

When one object slides over the surface of another, a frictional force is exerted in the opposite direction from which the object is moving. The purpose of this experiment is to evaluate some of the properties of friction and man's attempt to overcome them with the use of commercial lubricants: 10-20 motor oil, and oil additives.

Experimental Apparatus and its Function

The apparatus consisted of a wooden frame built to support a V-shaped ramp that was 150 cm long. The ramp was made from a 3 cm × 3 cm zinc-coated 90 deg angle iron mounted in the V-position. The sliding body was also a length of the same angle iron 4 cm long. This study will evaluate how these lubricants reduce the friction properties of a V-body sliding down a V-ramp; Fig. 1 presents a drawing of the apparatus.

My first effort was to determine the minimum slide angle with metal-to-metal contact. The angle was 16 deg and it was apparent that the sliding body accelerated as it moved down the ramp. Slide time was 2.0 sec, timed by a stopwatch. (Average of 10 trials with little range variance.)

I had thought that a liberal application of 10-20 motor oil on the ramp would *increase* the velocity and acceleration of the sliding body, but, to my surprise, it didn't! Oil viscosity *slowed* the descent time from 2.0 sec to 7.8 sec, with an erratic range of from 6.4 sec to 10.6 sec. It was apparent that there was little or no acceleration.

However, when I wiped the liberal quantities of oil down to an almost dry film, sliding time was decreased from 2.0 sec to 1.6 sec. (This represents an improvement in time efficiency of 20 percent.) I thought that perhaps the improvement in time might be the result of a polishing effect on the ramp because of usage, but the slide time stabilized to 2.0 sec again after the ramp and sliding body had been washed thoroughly with solvent and permitted to dry.

In two separate tests, I mixed individual additives with 10-20 motor oil (20 percent additive to 80 percent oil) and applied a thin film to the ramp. To my great surprise, the combined substance turned out to be very viscous and sticky. It would not permit the sliding body to move—even when the ramp was tilted to very steep angles. A summary of test data is presented in Table I.

The use of lubricants can improve the loss of performance caused by friction, but the lubricant must be the correct one for the individual situation, and must be properly applied. The thin oil film improved slide time by 20 percent over a dry metal-to-metal situation.

Although the oil additives did not work in this experimental situation, it is possible that they are valuable when applied to internal engines where high temperatures and other conditions may warrant their use, but I am not convinced of their value. Considerable experimentation, using real engines, would be required to evaluate their worth.

In the case of my ramp, perhaps a dry lubricant such as graphite or silicone spray might further improve efficiency. That possibility could also be the subject of additional testing.

Finally, remove the sentence part of your outline and insert the correct paragraphs under each heading to complete the report. Do not rewrite any paragraphs and use them all. Re-arrange paragraphs if necessary.

The operator is performing an extensive series of tests toward evaluating the efficiency of this front-end loader. He will write periodic reports on the testing, then a final report summarizing the findings.

CHAPTER 8

Preparing the Report

When the report writer has assembled and arranged his material according to an orderly plan or outline, he is then ready to begin preparing the various elements of the report according to this plan. The problem now is putting the words on paper.

Writing the First Draft

Suggesting to someone how to put words and sentences together in a report is much more difficult than pointing out the basic steps in report preparation, such as gathering the facts and planning the report. These steps are mechanical in nature and can be learned from a text. But actual writing of a report is more of an art than a science, therefore more is learned through practice than by reading specifications. Each writer has his own methods, which may work well for him but be completely ineffective for someone else. Consequently, the following suggestions are presented more to point the writer in a general direction rather than to specify exact methods.

Getting started is the first problem. Too many writers worry about getting an ideal opening. This only delays the actual start of the writing and is often extremely frustrating. The important thing is to *start*. It is best to put down the most appropriate opening that can be thought of at the moment and change it later if necessary.

Writing the textual elements first is a good idea, if not an essential one. Some elements, such as the Table of Contents and the Index, cannot be prepared until the text is written. Others, such as the abstract and the summary, are more easily prepared after the text is written.

Writing from the outline will help the writer see the stages in the material so he can concentrate on one stage at a time. Writing a long report can appear to be a highly difficult task unless the writer looks at it this way. The outline is prepared so that it can be used during the actual writing process. In essence, the writer enlarges the outline—by filling in the details—to complete the report.

Writing rapidly, without stopping to correct mechanical errors, helps the writer keep his train of thought. The editing will come later; the effort now is directed toward getting some facts and ideas on paper. Errors in spelling, punctuation, and grammar can be corrected after the first draft is finished.

Including more facts than are actually needed often helps the writer determine what is relevant and important and what is not. Most writers find it easier to go back and cross out material than to try to fill in the missing details.

Report Elements and Format

A report normally contains prefatory, textual, and supplementary elements. It is true that many reports do not have all of the elements covered in the following pages. As noted in Chapter 7 the most accepted report organization appears to be the scientific one, in which the writer states the problem, describes what was done, discusses the results, and presents the conclusions. These four parts are often the only elements used by a writer. Sometimes these elements are not actually distinguishable in the report, and some are not needed at all.

Yet, it should not be considered a waste of time to study all of the elements. Because in the longer, more complex reports most, or all, of the report elements may be needed. In this section the makeup of the different elements is presented.

They are discussed in the order in which they would probably appear in a report. However, the order is often at the discretion of the report writer, and the exact arrangement found here is not vital to the preparation of a good report. Elements of a report include:

REPORT ELEMENTS

Prefatory elements
    Transmittal letter (industrial use)
    Abstract (technical papers)
    Title page
    Foreword
    Table of contents (or Contents)
    List of tables (occasional use)
    Summary (occasional use)

Textual elements
    Introduction
    Discussion, or body of the report
    Conclusions and recommendations

Supplementary elements
    Appendixes
    Bibliography
    Distribution list (business and government)
    Index

Prefatory Elements

The transmittal letter, abstract, title page, foreword, table of contents, list of figures, list of tables, (sometimes, a composite contents page), and summary are presented here as the prefatory elements of a report. As the name implies, prefatory elements are those parts of the report that appear before the body or textual elements.

Transmittal Letter. The transmittal letter is used to transmit reports from the preparing organization to the recipient, or reader. It tells the recipient what the report is about. This includes presenting the subject of the report, authorization for its publication, and, if it is a periodic report, the inclusive dates that it covers.

The transmittal letter is usually typed on the letterhead of the organization that prepares the report. The brief body of the letter consists of short, simple sentences designed to permit the reader to know immediately what he has received. It is a business letter which can sometimes be more personal than the report itself.

In most cases each recipient should receive a transmittal letter with his copy of the report. It should be stapled or other-

Allen-Jones Steel Company
Salt Lake City, Utah 84145

January 18, 19--

Fourth National Bank
2 Henry Drive
Cambron, Idaho 83341

Attention: Mr. H.V. Mury

Subject: Building Construction Progress Report No. 1,
           Covering the period December 16 through
           January 15, 19--

Two copies of the report are submitted in accordance
with contract 2-068, dated September 8, 19--

                         Very truly yours,

                         Jackson R   Hamerton
                         Construction Manager

JRH/ej
Enc.;As stated.

Fig. 1. Example of a transmittal letter.

wise attached to the report. An example of a brief transmittal letter is shown in Fig. 1.

Abstract. The abstract presents briefly an explanation of the report content. Its importance to the reader, and therefore to the writer, can hardly be overstated. If properly written, the abstract provides a highly-efficient shortcut for those who wish to keep abreast of developments in their fields but have little time to wade through daily volumes of reports. It will tell the reader what he needs to know, or it will make it clear that he should read the entire report.

The abstract is important in another respect. Filed in a library, it becomes invaluable to researchers and other report writers who wish to learn what has already been done on a particular subject.

The abstract should seldom be more than one page long. The content should be limited to a brief explanation of what is discussed in the report and the conclusions reached. The material should be presented in the same order used in the report's textual elements.

As suggested previously in this chapter, the textual elements should be written before the abstract is composed. The writer then has a better grasp of what the report really covers and is in a better position to write the abstract. Fig. 2 shows an example of an abstract.

Title Page. The title page informs the reader of:

(1) Report title
(2) Publication date
(3) Report control number and copy number
(4) Contract number (if submitted in compliance with a contract)
(5) Period covered by the report (periodic reports only)
(6) Name of writer
(7) Name of person approving the report (if applicable)
(8) The agency for which the report is prepared

All of this information is important, especially for later reference that may be made to the report.

ABSTRACT

This report presents the results of a study to determine the optimum material to use in fabricating special production equipment for a new plant. The facts used in the study were obtained both from the material suppliers and from prior research data on some of the materials.

Those materials included in the study were:

Cast iron

Cast aluminum alloy

Malleable iron

Each material is rated as to its suitability. This rating is presented in tabular form, with a brief discussion of each material and its suitability or unsuitability for the purpose.

The results suggest that the optimum material, for all-around use in the new plant, is malleable iron.

Fig. 2. Example of an abstract.

Special emphasis should be placed upon the selection of a title. Although brief wording (less than eight words) is desired in a title, sometimes it is necessary to have a lengthy title to convey a complete understanding and to distinguish the report from others. If a report is to be filed—and most are—the title should be readily identifiable. This is why periodic reports should always have the dates covered on the title page, since the only item that will readily distinguish it from other reports in the series is the date or the report number.

The report control number, as the name implies, is used both by the preparing organization and the recipient to maintain control of the document. This number is also commonly used in maintaining a report filing system. The format for a title page is shown in Fig. 3.

BUILDING CONSTRUCTION

PROGRESS REPORT NUMBER 1

Prepared for:

Fourth National Bank
2 Henry Drive
Cambron, Idaho 83341

Prepared by:

Allen-Jones Steel Company
Salt Lake City, Utah 84145

Contract 2-068

December 16 through January 15, 19--

Prepared by:

H.R. Hamston
Construction Superintendent

Approved by:

Jackson R. Hamerton
Vice President

Fig. 3. Format for a title page.

Foreword. The foreword in a report should tell the reader:

(1) The reason for publishing the report
(2) Whether the report supersedes another
(3) Whether the report is preliminary, interim or final
(4) The period of time covered by the report (if it is a periodic report)
(5) The history of the problem discussed in the report

If the report contains company proprietary information, a proprietary information statement should be stamped or typed at the bottom of this page.

FOREWORD

This report is submitted by Allen–Jones Steel Company under Contract No. 2-069.

The contract covers the construction of a new building for the Fourth National

Bank. This report is the first in a series of monthly reports and discusses work

completed during the period December 16 through January 15, 19-- .

Proprietary Information

Information included in this report is confidential and should not be discussed

with unauthorized persons.

Fig. 4. Example of a foreword.

The foreword should contain short, simple sentences as shown in Fig. 4.

Table of Contents. If a report is longer than 10 or 15 pages and is divided into sections, some type of index is needed to guide the reader to those points that are of interest to him. This guide is usually in the form of a table of contents as shown in Fig. 5.

The entries in the table of contents also appear in the textual elements as headings or subheadings. Thus a reader is able to refer easily to a particular section or subsection of the report. Each heading in the table of contents must appear in the textual elements as a heading or subheading. However, it is not necessary that each subheading in the textual elements also appear in the table of contents.

The items in the table of contents are listed exactly in the order in which they appear in the report. The writer can complete the list of headings and subheadings as soon as he completes the rough draft. The page numbers cannot be added until the final draft is completed.

List of Figures. If the report contains five or more figures, a list of figures may be included.

TABLE OF CONTENTS

iv

Fig. 5. Format for a table of contents.

The list of figures shows the figure title, number and the page on which the figure appears in the report. Figures should be numbered consecutively with Arabic numbers and placed in the report as close to the textual reference as practical. The preparation of figures is discussed in Chapter 9. A format for a list of figures is shown in Fig. 6.

List of Tables. The list of tables lets the reader know the table title, number, and the page on which the table appears. It may be included in a report containing more than five tables.

LIST OF FIGURES

FIGURE NO.	TITLE	PAGE NO.
1	Retaining Wall Sketch	9
2	Culvert Sketch	10
3	Organization Chart	16

Fig. 6. Format for a list of figures.

LIST OF TABLES

TABLE NO.	TITLE	PAGE NO.
I	Structural Calculations	12
II	Manpower Utilization	15
III	Planned Manpower Utilization	17
IV	Estimated Labor Costs	18

Fig. 7. Format for a list of tables.

Tables should be placed in the text as close to the textual reference as practical, and should be numbered in order with Roman numerals. The preparation of tables is also discussed in Chapter 9. A format for a list of tables is presented in Fig. 7.

Composite Table of Contents. When the report contains only three or four tables and figures, the writer may choose to combine the list of tables, list of figures, and the table of contents as shown in Fig. 8.

Summary. The purpose of the summary in a report is to present a condensed version of the whole document. The summary should not merely outline the contents, as the abstract essentially does, but should provide a general reader with enough information so that he need not read further unless he wants to see complete details.

TABLE OF CONTENTS

FIGURES

TABLES

iv

Fig. 8. Format for composite contents list.

SUMMARY

This report presents the results of a study to determine the optimum material to use in fabricating special production equipment for a new plant. The facts for this study were obtained from material suppliers and from price research data on a number of the materials. The materials included in the study are:

(1) Cast iron

(2) Mallable iron

(3) Cast aluminum alloy

The factors used in determining the choice of materials are:

(1) Suitability

(2) Cost

(3) Delivery

Under the above general headings, another series of factors are considered, such as service life, mechanical loading, and weight. Using these factors as a basis, each material is rated as to its suitability. This rating is presented in Table IV, with a brief discussion of each material and its suitability or unsuitability for the purpose

The results suggest that the optimum material, for all around use in the new plant, is malleable iron.

ix

Fig. 9. Example of a summary.

Except for abnormally long reports, the summary should not be longer than one page. It is not an easy task for a writer to condense a long report into a summary that is only one or two percent of its length. The summary should include a statement of the problem, a brief explanation of the steps taken to solve the problem, and the conclusions and recommendations. This material should also be presented in the same order that is used in the report's textual elements.

A summary for a special study report might be written as shown in Fig. 9.

Textual Elements

The textual elements of a report include the: (1) introduction, (2) discussion and (3) conclusions and recommendations. These elements are where the reader actually finds out what has been done and what the results were. The reader looking for facts and detail finds them in these sections of the report. Fig. 10 shows a portion of an introductory page.

BUILDING CONSTRUCTION REPORT

PROGRESS REPORT NUMBER 1

1. Introduction

On November 1, 19--, the Fourth National Bank of Idaho entered into

a general construction contract with Allen-Jones Steel Company, Inc., to

erect a new bank building on the corner of 10th and J streets. Groundbreaking

was held on November 15, and construction work began on December 16. This

report states construction progress through January 15. All construction is

scheduled for completion by....

Fig. 10. Top portion of text page, showing introduction.

Introduction. The introduction must acquaint the reader with the report. It is here that he must be further introduced to the subject and to its purpose and scope.

The introduction should state the problem or project under

consideration and contain enough information to allow the subject to be discussed in the remainder of the report. This may include summarizing a history of the project and presentation of background information.

Some writers write the introduction before the remainder of the text. It may be easier, however, to write it after the other parts of the text are finished and while the material is fresh in the mind. The writer is more likely to cover all the necessary points in the introduction after having completed the discussion, conclusions, and recommendations.

Discussion. The discussion section contains the main part of the report. This is where the report writer indicates progress in meeting the purpose stated in the introduction. This part of the report must be complete, accurate and clear. This means that the purpose and reader must be kept in mind while writing.

Organization of this section is essential. The writer must avoid a rambling, disorganized discussion.

Content. The discussion is where the writer answers the *who, what, when, where,* and *how* of the subject. The *why* should have been answered in the foreword.

As in other elements of a report, the content of the discussion depends upon the type of report being written. Thus it is the writer's responsibility to determine what is applicable to a particular report. The amount of detail that should be included depends upon the subject, purpose and scope of the report. In some reports it is necessary to give every detail of the apparatus or procedure; in others, the discussion may be clear without such detail. The important point is that the writer should give the reader all the details required to understand the material.

Those reports that do require a lot of detail may also require the presentation of a mass of data. Often the numerical data cannot be presented in sentence and paragraph form. Tables are the appropriate form for presenting such data. Preparation of tables is discussed in Chapter 9.

Likewise, some details can be better presented through an

illustration. For example, an illustration (drawing or a photograph) is often used to show a setup for a test or experiment. Explaining such detail to the reader in sentences is often difficult and sometimes almost impossible. The preparation of illustrations is also discussed in Chapter 9.

Sections and Subsections. The discussion should be divided into sections and subsections according to the outline that evolves from organizing the material (Refer to Chapter 7). It appears that the trend in the modern report is to use smaller and smaller subsections. Dividing the report into sections and subsections enables the recipient to read only that part of the report with which he is concerned. It also provides the basis for a table of contents which enables the reader to obtain a rapid view of the content, arrangement and section location.

Although some progress reports are organized chronologically with subsections covering a certain part of the period, most reports are organized by topic. The topic type of organization is indicated by the table of contents example shown on page 125. The important point for the writer to remember is that the organization of the discussion element of the report should grow logically out of the subject matter and the requirements of the readers.

It is apparent that some means of identifying sections and subsections must be provided. This is accomplished by using headings and subheadings, respectively. Each heading should:

(1) Indicate the relative importance of the section it heads
(2) Be identical in form to headings of the same relative importance
(3) Be readily distinguishable from the order of other headings
(4) Be clearly distinguishable from text

Conclusions and Recommendations. The main contributions of the work are presented in the discussion element of the report. It has become somewhat standard practice, however, to bring these main contributions together and enumerate them in another element called conclusions and recommendations. A conclusion is an opinion based upon the results as stated in the report. A recommendation is a suggested course of action.

In some reports, recommendations are not required, and in some neither recommendations nor conclusions are required. For example, if the original problem as introduced earlier in the report has remained essentially unsolved, conclusions and recommendations can hardly be made. It is preferable to discuss the situation frankly and possibly suggest further research or other action. A section containing such statements is sometimes titled *Concluding Remarks*.

Generally those reports in which equipment or procedures are described, or those in which design data is merely tabulated, do not require conclusions and recommendations. Neither would *Concluding Remarks* be appropriate for such reports.

Conclusions and recommendations cannot be made in progress reports until the project is completed, unless it is possible to make conclusions and recommendations upon certain portions of the project before completion.

The decision as to whether to include conclusions and recommendations is not likely to be a major problem for the writer. The nature of the subject matter should suggest whether it is necessary or not.

Supplementary Elements

In most assignments, perhaps, the report writer does not need to include any supplementary elements. That is, the textual elements will usually be the last part of the report. Even so, in long, complex reports any one or more of these elements may be needed: appendixes, bibliography, distribution list and index.

Appendix. In some reports it is necessary to include bulky, detailed information to supplement the main discussion. Such information should be placed in an appendix. An individual report might contain several appendixes.

Information contained in an appendix should be only that which is indirectly related to the subject; directly related information should be part of the discussion. It must be decided whether such items as calculations, tabulated material, formulas, charts and photographs are essential enough to the reader's understanding to be included in the discussion. If not essential, they may be included as appendixes. This is sometimes an easy decision for the writer. Tabulated data, for example, can often be placed in an appendix because they have no direct relationship with the discussion; yet, they may be useful to the reader as a reference. The writer should decide whether the reader must look at the item (tabulated material, photograph, etc.) in order to understand what is being said in the discussion. If it is important, the writer must include the item in the discussion. However, it may still be desirable to put the item in an appendix if the reader must refer to it at a number of different places in the report. (This *Writing for Industry* has several appendixes.)

Bibliography. By definition, a *bibliography* is a list of writings relating to a given subject. A bibliography is useful in reports because it:

(1) Enables the reader to identify the material listed in the footnotes—see Footnotes discussion in this chapter (page 135)

(2) Directs the reader to sources of material used in the report

(3) Permits the author to acknowledge sources of information

The form of bibliographies has been essentially standardized to provide an efficient means of presenting the facts. Commonly used methods of presentation for a book and for a periodic publication are shown in Fig. 11.

In short bibliographies the items may be shown in one alphabetically-arranged list. If the author is unknown, the first key word (omitting *a, an,* and *the*) of the title is used in alphabetizing the list. The items in long bibliographies may be grouped by the type of material such as: primary sources, secondary sources, and works by an individual author.

Distribution List. A distribution list may be included as part

BIBLIOGRAPHY

BOOKS:

(1)   Steinberg, William B. and Ford, Walter B., Electricity and Elec-

tronics Basic, 4th ed. Chicago: American Technical Society.

PERIODICALS:

(2)   Doe, John J., "Vocational Writing," John Doe Journal, July, 19--

Fig. 11. Sample bibliography.

DISTRIBUTION LIST

BUILDING CONSTRUCTION

PROGRESS REPORT NUMBER 1

COPY NO.   RECIPIENT

1   Fourth National Bank
and   2 Henry Drive
2   Cambron, Idaho 83341
                                                Attn: Mr. H. V. Mury

3   Allen-Jones Steel Company
                                                Salt Lake City, Utah 84145
                                                Attn: Mr. K. R. Jones

4   R. A. Vamprant

5   C. M. Yaraman

6   R. V. Burr

Fig. 12. Format for a distribution list.

of a report which is going to be used by more than one person
or organization. The distribution list serves two purposes:
(1) it provides a means of controlling confidential information
in documents, and (2) it provides each reader with a list of re-

cipients. By referring to the distribution list, a person knows immediately who is responsible for safeguarding a particular copy of a confidential report. In addition, the recipient is made aware of associates who have copies of the report, therefore he can refer to it in correspondence and telephone conversations.

The distribution list should include the name of the recipient, address, and appropriate copy number as shown in Fig. 12.

Index. A report which contains 100 pages or more might need an index. This minimum size naturally depends upon the report content and the number of headings and subheadings. Some 40-page reports might also need an index.

The listing in the index should be in the same form that is used in the text. Headings and subheadings should be listed exactly as they appear in the text. Synonyms should not be used in the index.

A writer indexes a report by starting at the beginning and jotting on a note card each heading, subheading or any subject matter for which the reader might need to look. He also notes the page number on which each of the items appear in the report. He then alphabetizes the cards and has the index typed from them. Subsequently the typed index is checked with the report to make certain that all page references are correct. (See the Index at the back of this book for a typical example.)

Other Supplementary Elements. Additional supplementary elements occasionally given in reports include acknowledgements, list of abbreviations, glossary, and library cards. It is because of the generally infrequent need that these elements have been omitted from discussion in this book.

Footnotes

The report writer using material based upon the writings of others should acknowledge the sources. This acknowledgment shows the common courtesy of the writer and gives the reader the source of the material so that he may investigate further if he wishes.

Too many report writers use footnoting to such an extent that the entire presentation becomes awkward. There is no point in footnoting a fact which is well known. The writer must remember that footnotes interrupt the reader. He is not absorbing the material of the report when he stops reading to glance at footnotes. A writer should not include a footnote unless it is absolutely essential; such information can usually be put in the text itself.

Some writers prefer to list the sources in a bibliography in the back of the report. (See *Bibliography* in this Chapter.) This permits writers to include the sources without cluttering the text. A generally acceptable footnote style is shown in Fig. 13.

These tests were conducted to evaluate the variable-reluctance[1] of the system.

The quality of reproduction, when the electric signals were released from an amplification-speaker system, were measured to determine exact relationships. The tests showed an exact relationship between the quality of materials used in manufacture of the pick-up,[2] and the quality of the reproduction.

––––––––––––––––

[1] This principle is discussed in Electricity and Electronics Basic by Steinberg and Ford. (See Bibliography.)

[2] A pick-up is a device which can convert sound into electric impulses, e. g., a microphone.

4

Fig. 13. Footnote style.

Page Numbering

The important aspect of page numbering is that the number be placed in the same spot on each page. However, pages on

which a new section begins are counted but not usually numbered.

Writers have their own preference in the type and placement

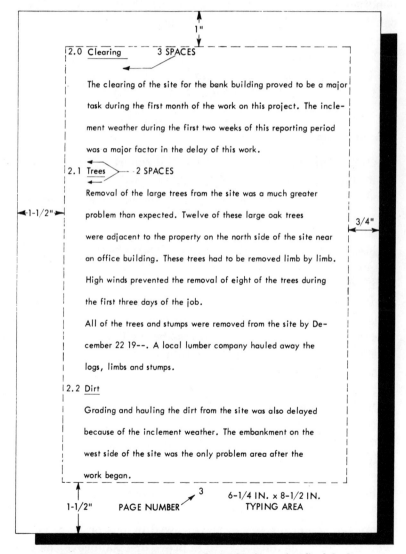

Fig. 14. Spacing, indention, and margins for typing final draft.

of the page number. The uncomplicated method of page numbering seems to be the one in which lower-case Roman numerals are used on the prefatory pages and Arabic numbers are used on all the other pages. Some writers, however, prefer to use an English letter with an Arabic number (such as *A-1*) for appendixes that have been designated by English letters. This can become a problem, especially when other elements follow the appendixes.

Centering the page number horizontally about ¾ inch from the bottom edge of the page is an acceptable location for most writing assignments. (See Fig. 14, page 137.)

The Final Steps

After completing the first draft, the report writer still has some important steps in his assignment before the report is finished. These steps, although not normally as time consuming as those covered before in this and prior chapters, are essential to distributing an acceptable report.

Editing the First Draft. Editing means checking the draft for errors, unimportant statements and omissions. In addition, editing is performed to ensure conformance to format, conventional word usage, and established style requirements. This general definition may fail to reflect the importance of this task. But neglect or carelessness here will almost certainly weaken the report. The best-written draft will need at least some editing before the final draft is typed. The techniques of editing are presented in Chapter 11.

Proofreading the Second Draft. The proofreading of the second draft, which has been typed from the completely edited first draft, is the next step in which the vocational report writer usually plays a major role. Proofreading means checking to make certain that no errors remain in the copy. (The techniques of proofreading are also covered in Chapter 11.)

Obtaining Necessary Approvals. When the report has been completed, generally it will be reviewed by one or more people who will have the authority to approve or disapprove the content. Many writers seem to consider these reviews to be completely unnecessary. Such attitudes are generally unwarranted. The writer's purpose should always be to make the report more readable and more accurate. Any step that helps in accomplishing these goals is worth while.

All comments and suggestions by the reviewers should be considered carefully. Some of them may be incorrect or may indicate that the reviewer has misunderstood some part of the report. If this happens, the writer should try to determine where the reviewer was misled. That part of the report may need to be revised. Being able to explain it satisfactorily to the reviewer will not suffice. The reader will probably not have anyone there to explain things to him when he receives the report. Thus, the writing itself must be clear.

Sometimes reviewers will make important contributions to the report. The writer should recognize and accept such contributions readily. The writer's responsibility to the reader should always be paramount.

The person, or persons, approving the report may wish to sign the report's title page. If the title page is not signed, it is customary to ask the reviewer to sign an approval form. This form can then be filed as proof that the approval was obtained before the report was distributed. If several changes are made to the report as a result of the review, these changes may have to be incorporated before the reviewer gives his approval.

Typing the Final Draft. When approvals have been obtained from the appropriate personnel, the final draft is ready to be typed on some type of offset plates, stencils, or bond typing paper from which copies can be made. It is important to check the approved draft carefully before it is retyped. Otherwise, errors may be overlooked and included in the final draft. The writer should see that all corrections and additions resulting from the reviews are included.

If the second draft is more than 20 pages in length, the final draft should be typed single spaced.

Correct spacing, indenting and ample margins are essential to a report's neat appearance, as shown in Fig. 14. As with most rules, deviations are sometimes necessary, but the writer should not deviate from standards if he can avoid it.

The typist may need additional instructions, depending upon the complexity of the job and her experience in typing similar reports. The writer should be prepared to give these instructions. He must also know—and tell the typist—how the report is to be duplicated so that the final draft can be typed on the correct stencil, offset printing master, or other duplicating material.

Proofreading the Final Draft. Proofreading the final draft is another of those tedious steps that most writers seem to deplore. It is a step, however, where neglect or carelessness can weaken or ruin a report that has been flawlessly researched and written. When a report is this near completion, it is obviously to the writer's advantage to make certain that this step is carefully completed.

Duplicating the Report. Although the report writer seldom duplicates his own report—even this can happen—he cannot simply drop the report at a machine and expect it to be duplicated without instructions. Whoever operates the equipment must know:

(1) Who ordered the copies
(2) The number of copies needed
(3) When the copies are needed
(4) Paper size
(5) Whether it is to be printed on both sides of the paper
(6) Whether the pages are to be collated
(7) Any special instructions: color, weight of paper, margins, etc.

There may be request forms on which these instructions can be written. If not, the writer should specify what he wants anyway, preferably in writing.

The writer must know, in advance, the equipment that will be used to duplicate his report. As explained before, this must be known before the final draft is typed. Large organizations often have full-scale print shops with a variety of equipment. Smaller organizations may have only one type of duplicating equipment.

Checking the Duplicated Copies. The reader who receives a report that is improperly put together or which has missing or illegible material is likely to have some doubts about the rest of the contents. Poor workmanship at any stage of report preparation raises questions in the reader's mind. The writer's attention to detail is no less important at this stage than earlier. Responsibility for the report—from beginning to end—belongs to the writer.

Errors can occur easily in the duplicating and collating process and they can go undetected. A report should not be delivered to the reader unless the writer checks the duplicated copies. It may not be necessary to check every copy; however, if there are only a few copies duplicated, checking every copy is probably a good idea. As a minimum, those copies should be checked that are going to the person or organization that requested or authorized the writing of the report.

The writer should make the quality control check of the copies to determine if:

(1) All pages are included and are right-side up
(2) All pages and elements of the report are in proper order
(3) All pages are legible

Distributing the Copies. The writer's job is finished, hopefully, after he has made certain that the report has been distributed in accordance with the already established distribution list. Distribution may be by hand delivery, inter-plant or inter-company mail service, or by U. S. Mail service. This depends, of course, upon the location of the recipient in relation to the person preparing the report and how soon the recipient expects to receive the report. Copies are frequently distributed both inside and outside the plant and company. The copy or copies are thus packaged and addressed accordingly. Reports which contain material classified by the U. S. Government must be distributed in accordance with special regulations.

Oral Reports

A few suggestions about oral reports are presented in this section. It is not intended to be a substitute for a course in public speaking. However, since oral presentation, or talking, is a very basic form of reporting on a subject, it deserves some mention in this text.

The oral report, as the printed report, is used to convey information. Hence, most of the material presented elsewhere in this book applies to both. The comments that follow are therefore limited to those that apply strictly to oral reporting.

Preparation. As it is true in the initial preparation of any report, an oral report is started by preparing an outline. The outline may be used to prepare a manuscript that will be read or memorized. Or the outline may simply be used as notes by the speaker to practice and deliver the talk.

The speaker should learn as much as possible about the subject. Even material that is not included in the speech itself may be useful in the question and answer period that often follows a speech. Knowing the subject thoroughly also gives the speaker the confidence needed in making a talk.

Deciding how to deliver the speech is important. It may be read, memorized or delivered off-the-cuff, using notes as needed. Delivering a speech off-the-cuff is desirable because it provides informality and naturalness which audiences prefer.

This does not mean, however, that presentations should never be read. Complex material that must be presented in an exact manner so that it can be clearly understood is often read. The speaker, in this case, tries to make sure that the material is interpreted in only the way that is intended.

The question as to whether a speech should be memorized becomes somewhat irrelevant as the preparation continues. Some speakers essentially memorize every word, while others concentrate on the main points of the subject and fill in the details as they make the speech. If the speaker is thoroughly familiar with the subject, it is not likely that he will forget anything important. The main points of the talk can always be written on small cards and used by the speaker during the talk without interrupting the informality and naturalness of the delivery. The possibility that a speech needs to be completely memorized is not likely.

As pointed out in previous chapters, a writer must always keep the reader in mind when preparing a report. Likewise, a speaker must keep the audience in mind when preparing a talk. It is known from experience that speeches can be very interesting, or extremely dull and boring. There are a variety of reasons for dullness and boredom, depending upon the individual speaker and the audiences to which he is speaking. One of the more frequent reasons, though, is the fact that a speaker often tries to cram too much detailed information into the talk. It is difficult for most audiences to long continue the deep concentration needed for detailed talks, thus boredom begins.

The material should be organized simply and logically so that the listener will grasp the presentation. As in report writing, the organization depends to a large extent upon the material to be presented and the audience.

The Audience and the Speaker. The speaker's relationship with the audience should be businesslike. The audience will consist of people who are seeking information about the subject and are not there for a show. The speaker should therefore make his talk directly and simply.

The speaker should look at the audience and be natural in posture. He should stand up straight, but not stiff. Movement around the speaker's area and gestures can be used to emphasize a point. Quick movements that distract the audience, however, should be avoided.

Perhaps the most important point that the speaker should remember in dealing with an audience is to be personable and natural. If a short story about some incident is needed to show this personable and natural attitude then it should be used. If the speaker begins by showing this attitude, the audience will usually be attentive and grasp the message from the beginning, which is exactly the speaker's goal.

Choice of Language and Presentation. Naturalness must definitely carry over into the choice of language used in a speech. Consider the following language:

> The work is held in a vise fastened to the top of a table. Fixtures may be used when justified by the quantity of items to be drilled. The fixtures may have T-slots and holes on the top surface and keys on the bottom surface in which to insert the center T-slot of the drill table.

These formal sentences might be used in a printed report, but using them as spoken material would demand too much concentration for listeners to maintain during the entire course of a speech. It is not natural for people to speak in this manner.

After years of practice in talking with others, a person develops a speaking style that is natural and that does not demand deep concentration on the part of the listener. This style is generally quite different from the printed report. Since the audience cannot re-examine any of the sentences or paragraphs that it does not understand, the speaker must make every thought clear enough to be understood the first time.

There should be no objection to a speaker expressing his own personality. And he should definitely not try to imitate anyone else's mannerisms or style of speech.

A speech is not merely a report that can be read or recited to an audience. Instead, it is a talk presented in the speaker's natural conversational style.

Visual Aids. Visual aids should be used when they contribute to the understanding of the material being presented. They should only be used to describe the work and only when they form a natural part of the presentation. Elaborate visual aids should not be used just for show.

Charts or slides may form an important part of the talk and they should always be presented with clarity. Just asking the audience to read the chart or slide is not enough. Using a pointer or his finger, the speaker should explain each item. As in other parts of the speech, the visual aids should not be cluttered with material not related to the exact subject. There would seem to be little point, for example, in showing a cut-away view of an entire engine when the subject pertains only to the engine's starter.

There is certainly no set rule for the number of visual aids to use. There are many factors to consider. The one rule that holds true for visual aids and the entire task of making an oral report is that the material should be presented clearly. Whatever is needed to accomplish this should be used.

EXERCISES

1. List the elements of a report and state their purpose.
2. Give two reasons why it is important to the reader that the discussion be divided into sections and subsections.
3. Write a brief explanation on how an abstract should differ from a summary of a report.
4. Choose a textbook from one of your technical courses and prepare a complete foreword for one of the chapters.
5. Why should the table of contents and the index be among the last parts to be prepared in a long report? What other elements are prepared among the last?
6. Make a survey of two businesses in your area to determine which duplication methods they have and which are used most often. Write a report to show what you learned from the survey. Include all prefatory and textual elements as discussed in this text.
7. From a recent trade journal, abstract an article on a technical subject.
8. Write a paragraph on what is meant by the statement: Writing is more of an art than a science, therefore more is learned through practice than by reading specifications.
9. Assume that the inspection of facilities at a manufacturing plant revealed the following:

    Administration building—four years old and in satisfactory condition

    Maintenance building—six years old and in satisfactory condition

Quality control building—seven years old and in satisfactory condition

Manufacturing building—22 years old

Heating system: Steam heating system is inadequate. Maintenance costs increased 12 percent last year over the previous year.

Lighting: Adequate except in the area of milling machines; two new fixtures are required.

Ventilation: Provided by windows; four additional exhaust ports needed for adequate ventilation.

Power: Supplied by local power company; supply is adequate.

Machinery: Most machinery is in satisfactory condition. However, maintenance costs on the three oldest milling machines have doubled in the past two years. These machines should be replaced.

Write an introduction for a report on this inspection.

10. Write a complete report on one of the following topics by obtaining material from a local plant, shop, or construction site. Supplement with facts from books or periodicals:

Modern welding processes	Trouble-shooting
New techniques in brick-	automobile
laying	electrical systems
Acoustic plasters	Machine shop layout
House modular construction	Safety in sheet metal work

11. Using the material obtained from books and periodicals mentioned in Exercise 10, prepare a bibliography.

12. Using the method suggested in this text, index a technical article from a recent trade journal.

13. Write conclusions and recommendations based upon the material shown in Exercise 9.

14. Why does footnoting deserve careful consideration?

15. Name the elements that you think would be needed in each of the following reports, explaining why each element would be essential:

Monthly progress report—25 pages

Final research and development report—110 pages

Safety survey report—52 pages
Weekly progress report—6 pages
Design study report—80 pages
Field trip report—2 pages

16. Check with a local printing establishment and determine what instructions they require with each job. If a request form is used, ask for a copy. Write a complete report on your findings. Do not forget to include conclusions and recommendations.
17. Why is a distribution list a good idea even for short, unclassified reports?
18. In your own words explain how writing from an outline helps the report writer do a better job.

This operator will change augers soon to drill some deeper holes in the ground. He will accidentally strike an underground power cable and cause a power outage. The operator had a map which showed the location of the power line, but the map was wrong! He will be required to write a report on the incident. That report will include such illustrations as the map with the wrong information, and one showing the true location of the buried cable.

CHAPTER 9

Illustration and Table Preparation

It has been argued that, in industrial and business situations, most facts can be communicated adequately with a drawing, diagram, graph, or table. Sentences and paragraphs are not really needed to tell the story. Occasionally, this argument is true, but experience has shown that both paragraphs and graphic presentations are usually necessary to tell the whole story properly:

OUTSIDE WALL CONSTRUCTION

Outside wall construction begins after the subflooring has been nailed (and glued) to the floor joists. Walls are made in sections of convenient length from $2'' \times 4''$ (2×4) framing lumber.

To improve fabrication efficiency, studs should be cut and stacked in sufficient quantity before actual construction begins. Studs should be $7'10''$ in length. When the thickness of two end plates (2 times $1\frac{1}{2}''$) are added to a stud height, overall wall height will be $8'1''$.

After the studs are cut, a jig should be built on the subflooring from 2×4 material to hold a wall height of $8'1''$.

Cut two 2×4's as top and bottom plates for the wall section. Try to make all sections 4, 8, 12, or 16' in length to permit efficient use of exterior sheathing material which is sold in 4' widths. Of course, not all sections can be made in these lengths, but these lengths are ideal.

Next, mark each plate with penciled double lines on 16" centers. Make the first interior stud center on 16" from the outside edge of the end stud. The double lines should be $1\frac{1}{2}''$ apart— the exact width of your 2×4 construction lumber.

Place the marked end plates in the jig, and insert all the studs in their proper 16" on-center positioning, as indicated by the pencil marks. If the jig has been made properly, the studs will fit snugly and will require a slight amount of force for insertion.

Then, nail the plate to the studs, using 16 penny smooth box nails. Two nails should be driven through the plate into each end of every stud.

After stud nailing is complete, a ¾″ fiberboard, waterproof sheathing is nailed to the top of the wall section work with 1½″ big-headed, galvanized roofing nails.

The wall section is then removed from the jig and raised to the upright position. It is nailed with 16 penny smooth box nails to its proper place along the outside edge of the subfloor.

Each raised section should be braced properly to prevent it from falling in a windstorm. Fig. 1 presents a flow diagram of the major fabrication steps.

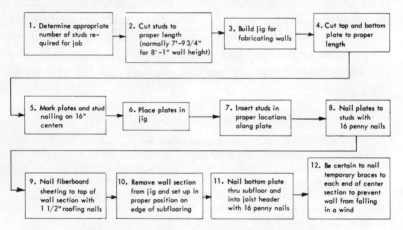

Fig. 1. Outside wall construction event sequence.

If the discussion of outside wall construction and the flow chart of steps in constructing the walls are read separately, they stand alone. One does not require the other for understanding. Yet together the two complement each other and tell a much better story. In this case the text is dominant over the figure, but a figure may often dominate the text, depending on the kind of information and the requirements of the reader. (For a carpenter, a floor plan says more than a chapter in a book.)

When you are writing a report, how do you know when to

include a figure or table? Mainly it is a matter of judgment.

There are four basic types of figures from which to choose: drawings, flow diagrams, photographs, and graphs. There are three table styles that may be selected: informal, open, or closed.

If you have a complex series of numerical data to display, perhaps it could best be illustrated in a closed table or graph (or both). If you're discussing a mechanism or an object, perhaps a detailed drawing or photograph is required to ensure that the reader understands what you're talking about. If you recall the screwdriver description in Chapter 5, it would have been much easier to communicate the actual description if a dimensional drawing or photograph had been included. Diagrams such as the example shown above are often used to explain manufacturing processes and other flow sequences. In some documents, photographic coverage is required as evidence that events depicted actually transpired.

All figures and tables should have a textual reference: ". . . as shown in Figure 34 or, Fig. 34." Figures should be numbered consecutively throughout a document in Arabic numerals. Tables are numbered consecutively with either Arabic or Roman numerals (Roman preferred). All figures and tables should have the components and characteristics discussed in the following outline.

Image Sizes and Page Arrangements

Since most industrial documents are ordinarily typed and reproduced on $8\frac{1}{2}'' \times 11''$ paper, a standard image size of $6\frac{1}{4}'' \times 8\frac{1}{2}''$ is suggested for all full page figures and tables.

Large illustrations may occasionally be printed on foldout pages within a given report. The standard page size for foldouts is $11'' \times 17''$. The figure image size is $18\frac{1}{2}'' \times 14''$. Foldouts should be used only when oversize figures are required to display details; foldouts are difficult to bind and are awkward for the reader to handle.

If your document is to be printed, it is best to prepare illustrations larger than the standard image sizes. Then they are photographically reduced to the correct size during the offset printing process. However, these figures cannot be drawn over-size with just any dimensions. Oversizes must be proportioned to the paper sizes. Fig. 2 presents a diagram showing useful oversize border dimensions for preparing figures. Fig. 3 presents a sample of a figure image area on an 8½″ × 11″ page.

Figures may be arranged on a page as full size, half size, or

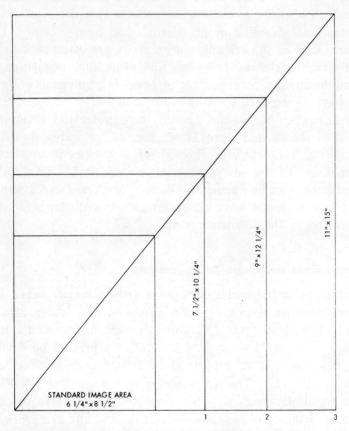

Fig. 2. Three useful border dimensions for preparing oversize figures. These oversize figures can be reduced to standard page size when printing operations are performed.

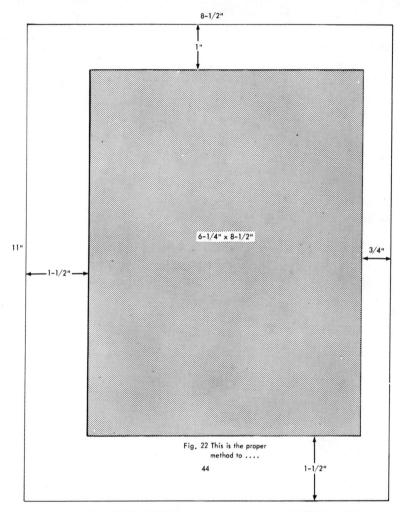

8-1/2"

1"

6-1/4" x 8-1/2"

11"

3/4"

1-1/2"

Fig. 22 This is the proper
method to ....

44

1-1/2"

Fig. 3. Sample of a 6¼" x 8½" image area on standard 8½" x 11" paper. Wider left margin is used to permit room for binding; wider bottom margin is used to allow room for figure title and page number.

quarter page as shown in Fig. 4. They may be either vertical or horizontal. Standard $8'' \times 10''$, $5'' \times 7''$ and $4'' \times 5''$ glossy photographs can be printed by an offset printing press using approximately the same reduced image sizes shown in Fig. 4.

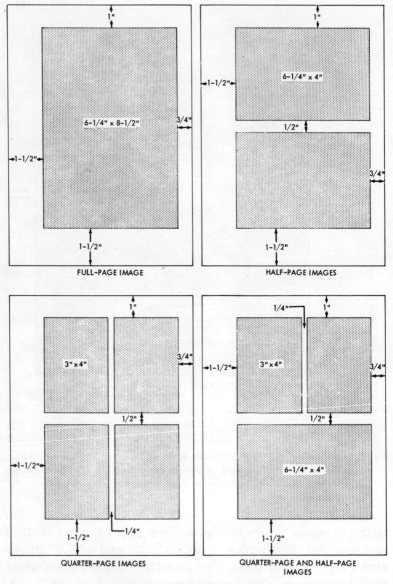

Fig. 4. Image arrangements for figures in a report.

Often, half-page and quarter-page figures are inserted on the same pages as text. Figures and tables should be inserted in the document as near to their point of textual reference as possible. For example, a full page table mentioned in the text on page 34 should appear on page 35, if possible.

Figure titles are centered under the image area. They may be short (2-3 words) or long descriptions. (See example under Outside Wall Construction discussion at beginning of this chapter and compare with title shown in Fig. 2.)

Consistency

To save expense, all lettering on figures for industrial reports should be typewritten. Lettering on oversize drawings may be typed on a wide-carriage typewriter, or drawings may be folded for insertion into the carriage. Lettering may also be typed on sticky-back paper[1] and affixed to the drawing. Lettering may be also placed on drawings by Leroy inking methods or by press-on systems,[2] but this work usually requires the services of a technical illustrator.

In a given document, line weights (thicknesses), letter sizes, and general appearance should reflect a feeling of consistency.

How to Prepare Figures

Drawings. Drawings are used primarily to show physical objects more clearly than can be demonstrated by words alone. Drawings can place special emphasis on certain parts or characteristics of an object that sometimes cannot be as effectively accomplished with words or photographs.

Drawings have five basic elements as shown in Fig. 5: (1) border line; (2) image (the item being portrayed); (3) callouts on the image (with use of arrows); (4) headings (over

---

[1]Chart-pak® and Avery Correction Tape are two trade names for sticky-back paper.

[2]Artype® is a trade name for press-on lettering systems. Many letter sizes and styles are available.

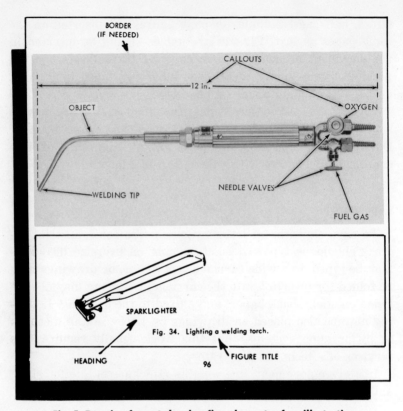

Fig. 5. Drawing format showing five elements of an illustration.

or under images) ; and (5) title (under the border area).

Unless you are artistically inclined or have a technical illustrator available to prepare your final draft illustrations, you may have difficulty in preparing the quality of work shown in the figures of this chapter. But don't let this fact discourage you. Most drawings in vocational and business reports are made with a typewriter and a ball point pen.[1] Certainly, if

---

[1]*American Technical Society's Freehand Sketching* is a valuable tool to aid the vocational writer who needs to make illustrations.

you have a complicated drawing to complete, and it is to be included in a very important document, you should enlist the services of a professional illustrator. But normally the ball point pen and typewriter method is sufficient.

When making a drawing (diagram or graph), prepare a rough draft of your proposed figure in pencil. Write a title, and include all necessary callouts and labels on the figure. Then read the text associated with that figure. Make any necessary improvements or corrections to the figure. Redraw the figure to the correct image size lightly in pencil, using such illustration tools as a protractor to determine proper angles, a compass to make circles, a French curve to make smooth curves, a ruler to make straight lines, and a triangle to make 90° angles. Then type in all lettering. Finally trace over the penciled lines with a ball point pen. Be certain to clean the tip of the pen before each line is drawn to prevent ink blobs from ruining your work. Make your work neat appearing and pleasing to the eye. The example diagram on exterior wall construction at the beginning of this chapter was drawn with a ball point pen and reproduced in this book via the offset printing process.

Flow Diagrams. Flow diagrams are a special type of drawing and are prepared in exactly the same manner as drawings. They may have all the general characteristics and components discussed under drawings, but they have the added feature of using little boxes with connecting arrows to indicate a flow pattern:

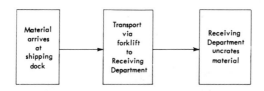

The example in the wall construction discussion at the beginning of this chapter is an excellent example of a flow diagram.

Photographs. Often, the writer is the only person who knows exactly what photo coverage is needed in a document. He may request the necessary photographs by telephone or letter from a company or other technical organizations.[1]

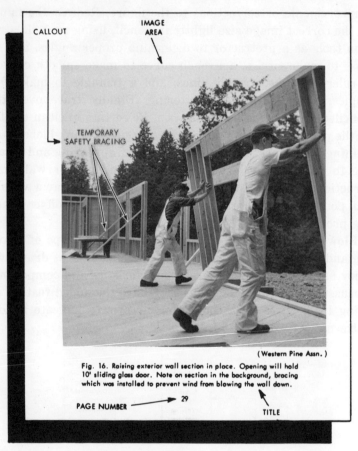

CALLOUT

IMAGE AREA

TEMPORARY SAFETY BRACING

(Western Pine Assn.)

Fig. 16. Raising exterior wall section in place. Opening will hold 10' sliding glass door. Note on section in the background, bracing which was installed to prevent wind from blowing the wall down.

PAGE NUMBER → 29

TITLE

Fig. 6. Paragraph format. Note that this figure does not conform to the recommended image size, but looks satisfactory anyway.

[1] Photographs and drawings obtained from someone else should not be used without permission.

If a photographer is employed at the same company where a writer works, the photographer may be asked to take the necessary pictures. A commercial photographer may be hired. Writers often take Polaroid pictures themselves to include in documents.

Photographic figures normally contain only two components: the image area and the title (description). But, photographic figures may also have callouts and headings typed on sticky-back paper and affixed to a thin, transparent plastic film which is then positioned over the photograph. Fig. 6 presents a typical photograph format.

Photographs are usually obtained in the 8″ × 10″ image size. They may be reduced to an image size approximately 6¼″ × 8½″ via the offset printing process.[1] As with any figure, photographs may be reproduced as half-page or quarter-page images; 8 × 10, 5 × 7, 4 × 5, or Polaroid 3⅜ × 4¼ images may be used in full-page, half-page, or quarter-page arrangements. Photographs may be ganged (grouped) on one page with separate figure titles or legends. However, the final printed image size of all photographs or ganged clusters of photographs should be approximately 6¼″ × 8½″. (See Fig. 4.)

Sometimes, photographs are inserted directly into a document in their original form. When this practice is necessary, the photographs should be glued (with rubber cement) to a sheet of 90 lb card stock. Titles may be typed on the card stock or typed on sticky-back paper and affixed to the card stock. Photographs may also be placed in transparent plastic folders for binding in documents.

Graphs. Graphs are drawings that show mathematical relationships. By seeing these relationships, readers can more readily understand statistical data better than tabular or text type presentations. Basic categories are the bar graph (Fig. 7), the circle graph (Fig. 8), and the line graph (Fig. 9). Graphs

---

[1] Before a photograph is reproduced, it is called a continuous tone image; after printing it is called a *halftone* because half of the grain in the photograph has been replaced with white area. The image on the half-tone is a series of little ink dots.

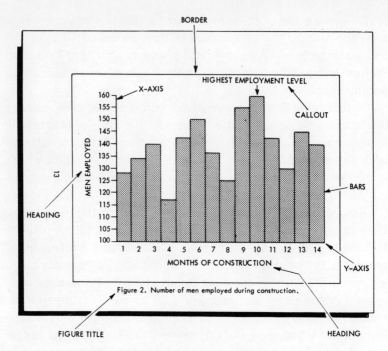

Fig. 7. Bar graph format.

are made using the same techniques and equipment discussed under drawing preparation.

A *bar graph* shows numerical relationships by presenting bars of various lengths to indicate values. Bars may be plotted on the X (horizontal) axis, as shown in Fig. 7 or on the Y (vertical) axis. Bar graphs contain seven components: (1) an X axis; (2) a Y axis; (3) bars; (4) border; (5) callouts; (6) headings; and (7) figure title.

If you were making a bar graph using the following data, it would be presented by the technique shown in Fig. 7. Notice that units on both the X and Y axes are drawn to a scale.

Example

The contract calls for the following number of men to be employed over a 14-month period, as follows: No. 1, 128; No. 2, 134;

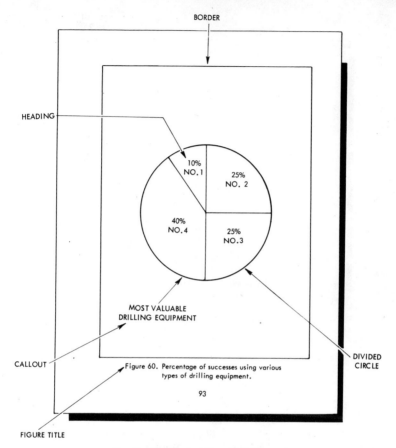

Fig. 8. Circle, or pie graph format.

No. 3, 140; No. 4, 117; No. 5, 144; No. 6, 150; No. 7, 137; No. 8, 126; No. 9, 155; No. 10, 160; No. 11, 145; No. 12, 130; No. 13, 145; and No. 14, 141.

A *circle graph* is used to present a percentage relationship between a part and a whole. Circle graphs contain 5 components: (1) divided circle; (2) headings; (3) callouts; (4) border; and (5) figure title. Consider the following data:

Example

We made a comparison of four drilling equipment types and compiled percentages of success using each type on an experi-

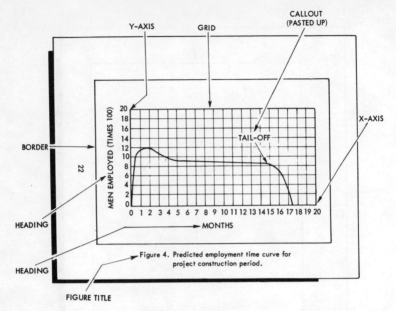

Fig. 9. Line graph format.

mental heat shield. Type No. 1 had 10 percent success; type No. 2 had 25 percent success; type No. 3 also had 25 percent success; and type No. 4 had 40 percent success and was selected as the most valuable type for this application.

The graphic display of this data is shown in Fig. 8.

To make a circle graph, each percentage must be related to 360° of a circle, and the angles plotted from the center of the circle must reflect that relationship.

To determine the relationship of a percentage to 360°, the ratio proportion formula must be employed:

$$\frac{360°}{100\%} : \frac{x}{10\%} = 36°$$

The following informal tabulation lists some circular degrees and percentage comparisons.

Percent	Center Angle (deg)	Percent	Center Angle (deg)
1	3.6	40	144.0
5	18.0	45	162.0
10	36.0	50	180.0
15	54.0	55	198.0
20	72.0	60	216.0
25	90.0	65	234.0
30	108.0	70	252.0
35	126.0	75	270.0

When making a circle graph, draw the circle and then use a protractor to plot the correct angles.

In *line graphs,* mathematical relationships are shown by means of a curve drawn on a grid coordinate system. (Some line graphs have an imaginary grid.) Line graphs contain seven components: (1) an X axis; (2) a Y axis; (3) a grid or imaginary grid (not drawn); (4) a curve that connects points on the grid (sometimes the curve is a straight line); (5) callouts; (6) border; and (7) a figure title. See Fig. 9.

The grid coordinate system is based on the following concepts. Numbers can be displayed as equal segments on a line:

Notice that each number has an equal space marked off on the line to represent its value. Both positive and negative numbers are represented. When the scale is drawn horizontally it is called an *X axis.* When the scale is drawn vertically, it's called a *Y axis.* When X and Y axes are combined, this forms the basis of the coordinate system:

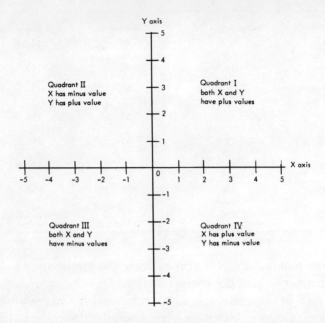

For example, if a point displayed on the coordinate system is X = +3, Y = +2, the point representing that value would be placed in quadrant I (A); X = −4, Y = −3 would be displayed as a point in quadrant III (B):

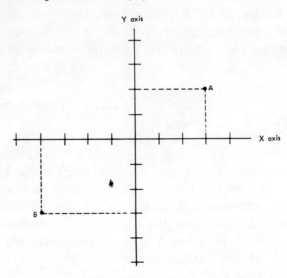

The dashed lines (preceding figure) are drawn in for clarification. Often the grid of the graph is imaginary as shown in the previous example. But grid lines can also be drawn as illustrated here:

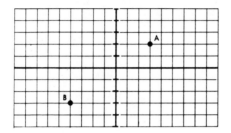

Ordinarily, only positive values for X and Y coordinates are displayed. Therefore, quadrant I is the most popular in use, and thus the other three quadrants are not shown in a figure. Consider the data in this paragraph:

In a 10-hour period, temperatures varied significantly at the construction site because of the passage of a storm front at approximately 4:30 p.m. Recorded temperatures are shown in the following tabulation:

	Time	Temperature ($^\circ$F)
(noon)	12:00	87
	1:00	88
	2:00	89
	3:00	89
	4:00	90
	5:00	60
	6:00	62
	7:00	58
	8:00	56
	9:00	58
	10:00	55

To graph this data, only quadrant I is required since there are no negative numbers. Let the X axis show time and the Y axis show temperature values. Points are placed on the imaginary grid, and straight lines are drawn to connect them. Note that sometimes curved lines are used instead of straight lines; individual points are not accentuated and thus become a part of the curve.

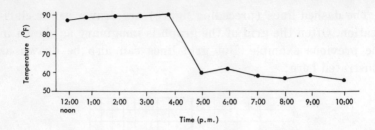

Fig. 9 presents a line graph with grid drawn in. Points are connected with a curved line and are not accentuated.

Tables

Tables, like figures, display numbers and facts in a more meaningful way than can be accomplished by paragraphing alone. The three types of tables ordinarily used in vocational reports and other documents include: the informal table, and the formal numbered tables, open (without lines) and closed (with lines).

An informal table is usually a short listing or comparison of data and does not have a table number assigned to it by discussion in the text. It may or may not have a title, and it may be either open or closed format. For example, test results are shown in the following tabulation:

QUALITY CONTROL RESULTS

Lot No.	Results	Lot No.	Results
131	Satisfactory	134	Satisfactory
131	Satisfactory	134	Satisfactory
131 A	Unsatisfactory	135	Unsatisfactory
131 B	No data	136	Unsatisfactory
131 C	Equipment failure	137	Unsatisfactory
132 A	Satisfactory	137 A	Satisfactory
133	Unsatisfactory	138	Satisfactory

Tables in a given document should be either open form or closed form, but not a combination of both. Format numbered tables in a given document should be consecutively numbered, using Roman numerals.

Table titles should be typed in capital letters; vertical and horizontal reference line headings can be either capitalized (Fig. 10) or initial capitalized. Asterisks or superscript lower case alphabet letters are used in tables to indicate footnotes.

Full-page tables should have a standard $6\frac{1}{4}'' \times 8\frac{1}{2}''$ image area. Tables which fill less than one page should be $6\frac{1}{4}''$ wide and any arbitrary length.

Oversized tables can be reduced to page size in printing operations, but they should be drawn with borders that conform to the image size shown in Fig. 2.

Formal open and closed form tables usually have four components: (1) title, (2) horizontal reference column (at the top), (3) vertical reference column (at the left) and (4) entries, as in Figs. 10 and 11. When you have a table to prepare, follow these steps:

(1) Select a title that describes the contents of the table in seven or less words

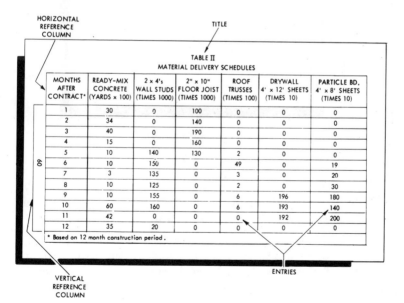

TABLE II
MATERIAL DELIVERY SCHEDULES

MONTHS AFTER CONTRACT*	READY-MIX CONCRETE (YARDS × 100)	2 × 4's WALL STUDS (TIMES 1000)	2" × 10" FLOOR JOIST (TIMES 1000)	ROOF TRUSSES (TIMES 100)	DRYWALL 4' × 12' SHEETS (TIMES 10)	PARTICLE BD. 4' × 8' SHEETS (TIMES 10)
1	30	0	100	0	0	0
2	34	0	140	0	0	0
3	40	0	190	0	0	0
4	15	0	160	0	0	0
5	10	140	130	2	0	0
6	10	150	0	49	0	19
7	3	135	0	3	0	20
8	10	125	0	2	0	30
9	10	155	0	6	196	180
10	60	160	0	6	193	140
11	42	0	0	0	192	200
12	35	20	0	0	0	0

* Based on 12 month construction period.

Fig. 10. Closed table format.

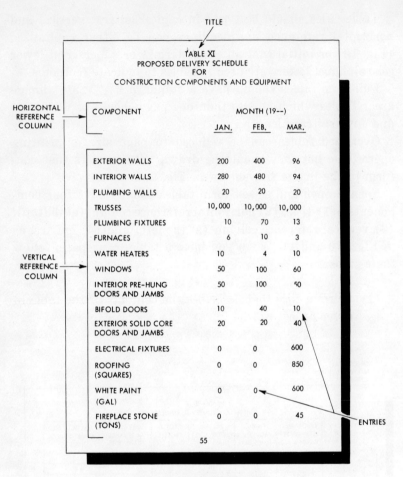

TITLE

TABLE XI
PROPOSED DELIVERY SCHEDULE
FOR
CONSTRUCTION COMPONENTS AND EQUIPMENT

HORIZONTAL
REFERENCE
COLUMN →

VERTICAL
REFERENCE
COLUMN →

COMPONENT	MONTH (19--)		
	JAN.	FEB.	MAR.
EXTERIOR WALLS	200	400	96
INTERIOR WALLS	280	480	94
PLUMBING WALLS	20	20	20
TRUSSES	10,000	10,000	10,000
PLUMBING FIXTURES	10	70	13
FURNACES	6	10	3
WATER HEATERS	10	4	10
WINDOWS	50	100	60
INTERIOR PRE-HUNG DOORS AND JAMBS	50	100	50
BIFOLD DOORS	10	40	10
EXTERIOR SOLID CORE DOORS AND JAMBS	20	20	40
ELECTRICAL FIXTURES	0	0	600
ROOFING (SQUARES)	0	0	850
WHITE PAINT (GAL)	0	0	600
FIREPLACE STONE (TONS)	0	0	45

ENTRIES

55

Fig. 11. Open table format.

(2) Set up horizontal and vertical reference columns by writing in a description of data to occur in those columns

(3) Insert comparative entries in the body of the table

For example, Figs. 10 and 11 present the two delivery schedules of elements for a large home construction project. How do you set up such tables? Well, you know that you will be comparing delivery of individual materials and equipment against a monthly schedule. So you can list the number of months of expected deliveries in the vertical reference column and the items to be delivered in the horizontal, or vice versa. Then write in the proper entries.

EXERCISES

1. What is the value of a drawing or a table in a written document?
2. When you are writing a report, how do you know when to include a figure or table?
3. What is the image size for: (a) full-page $8\frac{1}{2}'' \times 11''$ format; (b) half-page format?
4. What is meant by the suggestion that all tables and figures should have a *textual reference?*
5. If you were writing a report and the contents of a half-page table were discussed on the top half of page 34, where would you insert your table in the text?
6. What are Chart-pak and Artype?
7. List several tools useful for making illustrations and tables.
8. List components of:
   a. Photographic figures
   b. Drawings
   c. Flow diagrams
   d. Graphs
      (1) Bar graphs
      (2) Circle graphs
      (3) Line graphs
   e. Tables
9. Discuss the characteristics of two types of tables.
10. Write a procedure to change a tire on an automobile. Make two drawings a part of your write-up.
11. At the beginning of this chapter there is a flow diagram showing outside wall construction steps. Using a ball-point

pen, try to redraw and improve this diagram. (Hint: read the text associated with the drawing.)

12. In a write-up no longer than two pages, explain what the coordinate grid system is. Use illustrations to make your description clear.

13. These points are to be plotted in quadrant I of a coordinate grid system: $X = 1$, $Y = 9$; $X = 2$, $Y = 7$; $X = 3$, $Y = 5$; $X = 4$, $Y = 3$; $X = 5$, $Y = 1$; $X = 6$, $Y = 3$; $X = 7$, $Y = 5$; $X = 8$, $Y = 7$; and $X = 9$, $Y = 9$. After the points are plotted, connect them with straight lines. Use an imaginary grid format.

14. Consider the following temperature-time data:

Time	Temp (°F)	Time	Temp (°F)
1:00 a.m.	−10	10:00 a.m.	+32
2:00 a.m.	− 5	11:00 a.m.	+32
3:00 a.m.	− 1	12:00 noon	+32
4:00 a.m.	− 1	1:00 p.m.	+28
5:00 a.m.	0	2:00 p.m.	+26
6:00 a.m.	+10	3:00 p.m.	+32
7:00 a.m.	+20	4:00 p.m.	+22
8:00 a.m.	+32	5:00 p.m.	+21
9:00 a.m.	+34	6:00 p.m.	+20

Plot this data in a coordinate graph using a quadrant I and IV combination.

Snow falls on this day when the temperature is about 32°F. Put a callout on your graph showing the point in time when snowfall probably started and another which shows when snowfall probably ended.

15. A small construction company budget of $106,261.60 has the following characteristics:

    a. 23% wages to production personnel

    b. 12% wages to office personnel

    c. 10% rent

    d. 27% material costs

    e. 13% shipping costs

    f. 15% miscellaneous expense

Draw a circle graph showing dollar expenditures for that company.

16. Fig. 9 shows predicted manpower requirements for a construction project. Using this figure, prepare an informal table of the data.

17. Fig. 10 is a table listing delivery schedules for materials at a construction project. Draw a line graph plotting the ready-mix concrete delivery schedule.

18. Using data from Fig. 10, draw a bar graph showing particle board delivery from the 6th through 11th months of the construction project.

19. You have seen highway department personnel making traffic surveys. Go to a busy intersection which is equipped with a signal light. Make a survey of cars for each direction, then write a report on it. Your report should include a drawing, a table, and a graph. It should also include your written conclusions.

As you work in your employment specialty you will receive advancements and promotions. And as you accept this additional responsibility, you will be required to do more writing. Reports, business letters, instructions, specifications and other documents must be prepared and approved by management. The hydraulic grader shown here is engaged in an extensive road building project. Construction progress reports must be written for this program.

CHAPTER 10

Forms for Specific Reports

We have covered the elements and formats that are used primarily in lengthy, more formal reports in Chapter 8. As indicated in that chapter, however, the commonly prepared reports seldom have all the elements or the exact form covered there. In fact, often the short-form reports prepared by vocational writers may need only two or three of those elements. Thus the form varies according to the type of report.

In this chapter, a number of the more common types of reports are discussed. The forms presented here are not the only ones that could be used for specific reports. The exact form, if not already specified, should always be chosen after the writer has given careful consideration to his subject, the purpose for which the report will be used, and the reader.

Letter Reports

When the report contains not more than two or three pages, often it is presented in the form of an ordinary business letter. Actually, all report writing conforms more or less to the manner of the ordinary letter.

The modern report, as noted earlier in this text, is a type of writing that has developed a style and form in keeping with the demands of the streamlined methods of industrial operations that are in use today. It is written for definite and practical ends. It is not necessarily written for the pleasure of the reader or the writer. The aim is to give enough information clearly and concisely. A letter report is often the best form for the writer to use in doing this.

The most noticeable difference between modern business letters and reports is the evidence of a personal tone in the letters. The writer of letters often makes use of pronouns such as "I" and "you." A report, however, is mainly impersonal and is thus objective in tone. The information in the report is the important factor—not the personal relationship between the writer and the reader. Yet the trend today is to subordinate the personal relationship but not ignore it completely. Modern letter reports often have a personal tone.

The letter report form provides the writer with a means of presenting information in a personable, courteous manner. Although this is often very desirable, it does not mean that the writer should load the letter report with flowery words. The letter report, like other report forms, should cover the subject and then stop. The writer should not include material that is not needed.

Letter Styles. The three basic letter styles that are prepared in modern organizations are the modified block style, the full block style and the indented style. Three letters, with identical content, that have been typed in these respective styles, are shown in Figs. 1, 2 and 3. The most popular format is the modified block style. The full block and the indented styles are about equal in popularity. The trend appears to be toward increased use of the full block style because it is easier to prepare than the others. This style eliminates the typing motions required for indentions and positioning, since all components are typed flush against the left margin.

The characteristics of the three letter styles are:

Modified Block Style. (1) the date line is approximately even with the right margin; (2) The paragraphs are full block style; (3) The complimentary close and signature lines are five spaces right of center.

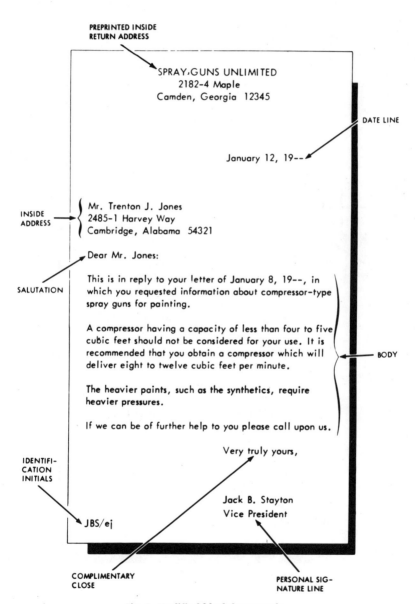

PREPRINTED INSIDE
RETURN ADDRESS

SPRAY₅GUNS UNLIMITED
2182-4 Maple
Camden, Georgia 12345

DATE LINE

January 12, 19--

INSIDE ADDRESS

Mr. Trenton J. Jones
2485-1 Harvey Way
Cambridge, Alabama 54321

Dear Mr. Jones:

SALUTATION

This is in reply to your letter of January 8, 19--, in which you requested information about compressor-type spray guns for painting.

A compressor having a capacity of less than four to five cubic feet should not be considered for your use. It is recommended that you obtain a compressor which will deliver eight to twelve cubic feet per minute.

BODY

The heavier paints, such as the synthetics, require heavier pressures.

If we can be of further help to you please call upon us.

Very truly yours,

IDENTIFI-
CATION
INITIALS

Jack B. Stayton
Vice President

JBS/ej

COMPLIMENTARY
CLOSE

PERSONAL SIG-
NATURE LINE

Fig. 1. Modified block letter style.

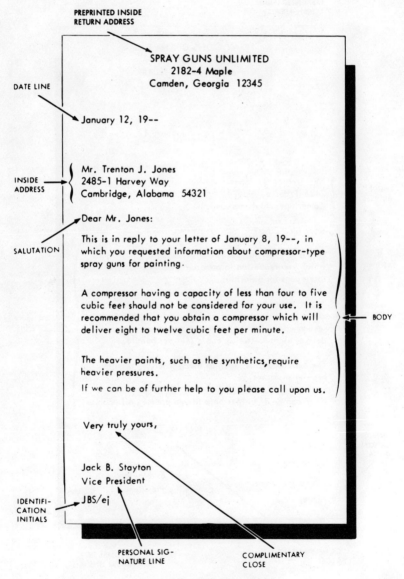

PREPRINTED INSIDE
RETURN ADDRESS

DATE LINE

INSIDE
ADDRESS

SALUTATION

BODY

IDENTIFI-
CATION
INITIALS

PERSONAL SIG-
NATURE LINE

COMPLIMENTARY
CLOSE

SPRAY GUNS UNLIMITED
2182-4 Maple
Camden, Georgia 12345

January 12, 19--

Mr. Trenton J. Jones
2485-1 Harvey Way
Cambridge, Alabama 54321

Dear Mr. Jones:

This is in reply to your letter of January 8, 19--, in
which you requested information about compressor-type
spray guns for painting.

A compressor having a capacity of less than four to five
cubic feet should not be considered for your use. It is
recommended that you obtain a compressor which will
deliver eight to twelve cubic feet per minute.

The heavier paints, such as the synthetics, require
heavier pressures.

If we can be of further help to you please call upon us.

Very truly yours,

Jack B. Stayton
Vice President

JBS/ej

Fig. 2. Full block letter style.

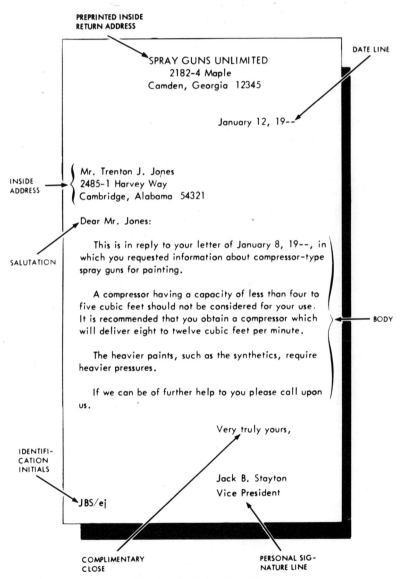

PREPRINTED INSIDE
RETURN ADDRESS

DATE LINE

SPRAY GUNS UNLIMITED
2182-4 Maple
Camden, Georgia 12345

January 12, 19--

INSIDE
ADDRESS

Mr. Trenton J. Jones
2485-1 Harvey Way
Cambridge, Alabama 54321

Dear Mr. Jones:

SALUTATION

This is in reply to your letter of January 8, 19--, in which you requested information about compressor-type spray guns for painting.

A compressor having a capacity of less than four to five cubic feet should not be considered for your use. It is recommended that you obtain a compressor which will deliver eight to twelve cubic feet per minute.

BODY

The heavier paints, such as the synthetics, require heavier pressures.

If we can be of further help to you please call upon us.

Very truly yours,

IDENTIFI-
CATION
INITIALS

Jack B. Stayton
Vice President

JBS/ej

COMPLIMENTARY
CLOSE

PERSONAL SIG-
NATURE LINE

Fig. 3. Indented letter style.

Full Block Style. All components are typed flush with the left margin.

Indented Style. (1) The date line is approximately even with the right margin; (2) The paragraphs are indented; (3) The complimentary close and signature lines are five spaces right of center.

Letter Components. Letters have eight basic components, but may have as many as nineteen. First, the eight basic components are:

(1) Inside return address—company letterhead stationery usually serves this purpose
(2) Date line
(3) Inside address
(4) Salutation
(5) Body of letter
(6) Complimentary close
(7) Personal signature line
(8) Identification initials of person dictating or writing and the typist or secretary

Figs. 1, 2 and 3 have these eight components. When necessary, letters may also contain any of these additional components:

(9) Mailing notation
(10) Personal or company confidential notation
(11) Attention line
(12) Subject line
(13) Reference line
(14) Subsequent page reference line
(15) Company signature line
(16) Enclosure list
(17) Carbon copy notation
(18) Postscript
(19) Letter reference number

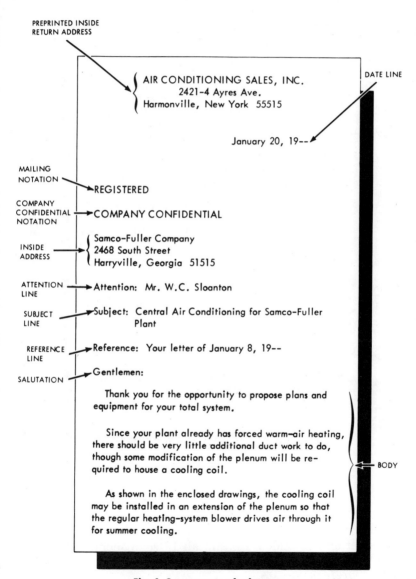

PREPRINTED INSIDE
RETURN ADDRESS

DATE LINE

AIR CONDITIONING SALES, INC.
2421-4 Ayres Ave.
Harmonville, New York 55515

January 20, 19--

MAILING
NOTATION

REGISTERED

COMPANY
CONFIDENTIAL
NOTATION

COMPANY CONFIDENTIAL

INSIDE
ADDRESS

Samco-Fuller Company
2468 South Street
Harryville, Georgia 51515

ATTENTION
LINE

Attention: Mr. W.C. Sloanton

SUBJECT
LINE

Subject: Central Air Conditioning for Samco-Fuller
Plant

REFERENCE
LINE

Reference: Your letter of January 8, 19--

SALUTATION

Gentlemen:

Thank you for the opportunity to propose plans and
equipment for your total system.

Since your plant already has forced warm-air heating,
there should be very little additional duct work to do,
though some modification of the plenum will be required to house a cooling coil.

BODY

As shown in the enclosed drawings, the cooling coil
may be installed in an extension of the plenum so that
the regular heating-system blower drives air through it
for summer cooling.

Fig. 4. Components of a letter.

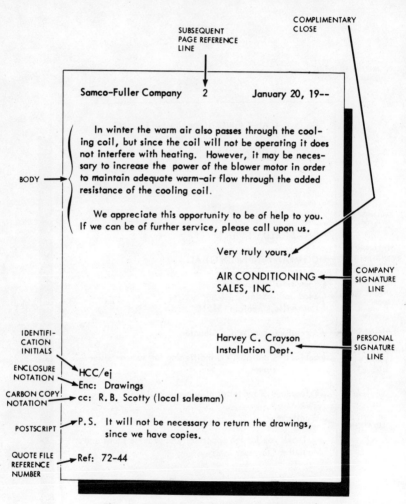

Fig. 4. Components of a letter, (cont.)

One letter will seldom contain all 19 components. However, for illustration purposes only, Fig. 4 shows a two-page letter which contains all of them.

Use of Letter Reports. The letter report can serve many purposes. It can be used for almost any type of reporting that is required, although it may not always be the best one to use. In fact, the letter report form could be substituted for many of the report forms to be studied in the following sections of this chapter. It is well worth the effort, however, for the writer to know about the other forms so that he is able to choose the best for his particular need.

Memorandum Reports

Within many organizations the memorandum is the most widely used report form. It is usually restricted to distribution within the same company.

MEMORANDUM

March 4, 19--

TO: Safety Department

FROM: J.W. Millison, Carpenter Shop

SUBJECT: Investigation of Accidents on Shop Jointers

The accidents on jointers in the plant carpenter shop have been caused by jointing small pieces without the use of jigs to hold the work and thus keep the hands away from the knives.

It is therefore recommended:

(1) That proper jigs be made and put in at once.

(2) That this be the subject of the next carpenter shop monthly safety meeting.

Fig. 5. Example of a half-page memorandum report.

It is essentially an informal type of communication between employees of the same organization.

Although the purpose of the memorandum report is basically the same as that of the letter report, they differ somewhat in style. The primary function of the style is to save the time of both the reader and the writer. Courtesy is generally sacrificed for conciseness since the writer and reader probably know each other. For example, *To* and *From* are used instead of a salutation and a complimentary close.

A half-page memorandum, as shown in Fig. 5, is quite common. Frequently, organizations will use both this size and a full-page size, depending upon the length of the report.

Investigation Reports

Investigation reports, although based on and closely related to facts, are at least in part opinion reports. This is true because the investigation from which conclusions and recommendations are drawn often involves comparing the subject with other similar things. As learned earlier in this text, conclusions and recommendations are opinions of the writer but hopefully have been drawn from concrete facts. Investigation reports, then, may contain a lot of facts and are close to factual, but they are not entirely factual because opinions different from those drawn in the reports are often possible.

At the end, an investigation report answers such questions as: "Is it fit for use? Is it effective or ineffective? What is it worth? Is it the best equipment for our use?" These questions are answered by making judgments about the facts that the writer has available.

For example, the vocational writer may be assigned the job of investigating and reporting on the possibility of using a particular piece of equipment in a machine shop. The writer, of course, needs to compare the new piece of equipment with similar equipment already used in the shop and possibly that used by other shops in the area. He may also want to compare several new pieces of equipment made by different manu-

INVESTIGATION REPORT

1. Summary

2. Introduction

3. Details of the investigation

4. Conclusions and recommendations

Fig. 6. Outline for a brief investigation report.

facturers. Finally, the writer must apply a standard based on facts about what a satisfactory piece of equipment might be.

Much of the material in investigation reports is specific detail, but obviously the subject may demand summaries of facts, interpretations, and evaluations, all made by the vocational writer. As in several other types of reports discussed in this chapter, the form of the investigation report may vary considerably, depending upon the nature and complexity of the subject. A brief outline for an investigation report is shown in Fig. 6. The outlines in Chapter 7 on the "Design and Fabrication of Inspection Equipment" (pages 107-109) are examples of an investigation report form for longer reports.

Inspection Reports

A vocational writer is sometimes confronted with the job of inspecting an object or situation and reporting back to someone on the result of the inspection. He may be acting as part of a team assigned to perform the inspection and make the report, or he may handle the job alone.

MEMORANDUM

July 18, 197-

TO: Henry Saco

FROM: Harold Sattles

SUBJECT: Inspection of Prototype Cylinder, Serial No. 12

The cylinder was inspected on this date. The following measurements were taken in the order listed:

1. The outside diameters at the top, bottom and middle were measured and recorded. An outside micrometer was used in taking these measurements. The recorded dimensions were:

    Top   1.421 in.

    Bottom   1.422 in.

    Middle   1.421 in.

2. The length was measured using an outside caliper. The recorded dimension was 2.512 in.

3. The wall thickness was measured at three places, 120 degs. apart, at each end of the cylinder. An outside micrometer with a ball attachment was used in taking these measurements. The recorded dimensions were:

    Top   0.031, 0.032, 0.031 in.

    Bottom 0.032, 0.031, 0.031 in.

The weight of the cylinder was 0.20 pounds.

A visual inspection of the cylinder showed that there were no irregularities on the machined surfaces.

Fig. 7. An example of an outline for an inspection report on a fabricated small part.

BUILDING INSPECTION REPORT

1.　Introduction (purpose of inspection and general statement about the structure)

2.　Type of construction

3.　Lighting

　　A. Type

　　B. Adequacy

4.　Heating

　　A. Type

　　B. Adequacy

5.　Plumbing

6.　Flooring

7.　Roofing

8.　Workmanship

　　A. Outside

　　B. Inside

9.　Landscaping

10.　Conclusion and recommendations

Fig. 8. An example of an outline for a building inspection report.

There are so many different types of inspections that any effort to classify the types of reports to cover them is almost hopeless. The vocational writer, consequently, must often use his own knowledge in devising a report form to fit his particular needs. He should remember, though, that following standard practices wherever possible usually saves the reader time and effort.

The items inspected and reported on can range from a small fabricated part to a large building to an entire operating plant. In the case of a report on the inspection of a small part, such as a cylinder, the report may be in the form of a memorandum as shown in Fig. 7. However, the report on the inspection of a building to determine its usefulness to house a production plant may take a considerably different form. An outline that might be used for this type of report is shown in Fig. 8.

Recommendation Reports

Any report that contains recommendations could in a broad sense be called a recommendation report. As you have learned, many reports contain recommendations.

As in the investigation report, the content of a recommendation report is mostly explanation of the data and description of the materials or objects involved. Also, as in the investigation

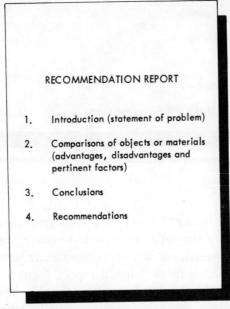

Fig. 9. An example of a recommendation report outline presented in the order in which facts were gathered.

SELECTION OF MACHINERY

1. Introduction (statement of problem)
2. Summary
    2.1 The type selected (recommendations)
    2.2 Brief reasons for the selection
3. Standards (which the machinery must meet)
4. Comparisons
    4.1 Type A
    4.2 Type B
    4.3 Type C
    4.4 Type D
5. Description of machinery selected

Fig. 10. An example of an outline for a recommendation report on the selection of a new piece of machinery.

report, the order in which the facts were obtained may or may not be the order of the written report. The writer's objective in the recommendation report is to lead the reader gradually to the same opinion that the writer holds. Whatever form produces this result is the one that should be used. There is obviously no standardized form that can do this in every situation.

In some instances, the writer may decide that the natural form for the report is in the order in which he gathered the facts or conducted the investigation. Frequently, this is the normal order in which the mind works in accepting a recommendation for taking action. Therefore, it is equally effective for the writer. An outline for such a report form is presented in Fig. 9.

In other cases, the writer may find that he can best present the material in the form shown in Fig. 10, which is an outline for a report on the selection of a piece of machinery.

The basic problem that faces a writer of recommendation reports is what form to use to make the logic of your recommendations clear to the specific readers. The solution to this problem is likely to vary, as indicated before, from report to report.

Equipment Failure Reports

Repairs and delays caused by equipment failures are very expensive when modern, complex machinery is involved. Such machinery as large, earth-moving vehicles used in the construction industry, and computerized lathes that are used in many factories today are examples of this equipment. If such equipment fails to operate properly, management must find out what caused the failure, get the equipment back in operation, and try to prevent future failures.

It is sometimes necessary to prepare written reports on the failure of equipment. This type of report may have many names, such as *Equipment Failure Report* or *Breakdown Report*. It is used to document the details of the failure. These details can be used to investigate and hopefully to prevent such failures in the future.

The vocational writer preparing an equipment failure report should simply explain what occurred. Was the operator following the operating procedures? What were the operating conditions at the time? Was human error involved? These are the type of questions that should be answered in the report.

Fig. 11 shows an example of a form that might be used for equipment failure reports. Fig. 12 is an example of an outline that might be used for those equipment failure reports that require more narrative explanations.

Specification Sheets

The vocational writer may be called upon to prepare a specification sheet for a manufactured item. As the name implies,

Report number: Date:

Equipment identification:

Equipment serial number:

Location of equipment:

Date of failure: Category of failure:

                                        Critical   ( )

                                        Major   ( )

                                        Minor   ( )

Description of failure:

Disposition and recommended corrective action:

Number of similar failures: Action to be taken by:

Reported by:

Fig. 11. An example of an equipment failure report form.

specification sheets are used to specify, in writing, the requirements that an item must meet.

The specification sheet is, again, one of those report forms that can be as varied as the item it covers, so the form shown

EQUIPMENT FAILURE REPORT

1. General description (of the failure)

2. Pertinent facts (condition which could have contributed to the failure)

3. Account of the failure (what happened)

4. Corrective action taken immediately

5. Conclusion and recommendations

Fig. 12. Example of an equipment failure report outline.

in Fig. 13 is only one of many that could be used. Others that the writer may devise may be just as effective, or more so, for his purpose.

The top portion of the specification sheet shown in Fig. 13 identifies the document and gives its date of effectivity. The first column in the body of the specification sheet simply shows the item number in the order that each should be inspected. The dimension description tells the reader what part of the item is to be inspected. The specification column is where the requirements are given. If these are dimensional requirements, minimums and maximums are shown. A dimension outside these limits rejects the item for the specified use. The inspection method column tells the reader how the item is to be inspected. In the example, the type of instrument is given in some instances. The word *gage* means that a specially designed gage is used in taking the measurement. In the example, the workmanship is visually checked.

A complex specification for a material or a mechanical item may contain six sections. These are: (1) scope, (2) applicable documents, (3) requirements, (4) quality assurance provisions, (5) preparation for delivery and (6) notes. Generally, the contents of each section are as follows:

SPECIFICATION SHEET

No. 10-4

Part Name:	<u>Flow Reducer</u>	Project:	<u>Furnace Instl.</u>
Part No.	<u>24-122814</u>	Drawing No.	<u>14902</u>

Item No.	Requirement Description	Specification (inches)	Inspection Method
1	Length	4.95 / 4.91	Gage
2	Outside diameter--top	1.58 / 1.55	Gage
3	Inside diameter--top	1.02 / 1.00	Gage
4	Inside diameter-- first step	1.24 / 1.21	Gage
5	Inside diameter-- second step	1.32 / 1.29	Gage
6	Outside diameter-- bottom	1.88 / 1.85	Gage
7	Inside diameter-- bottom	1.32 / 1.29	Gage
	Workmanship: check for smooth surfaces inside and outside	Must be free of gouges inside	Visual
	Notes:	No gouges more than 1/8" allowed outside	

Fig. 13. An example of a specification sheet.

Scope. The scope briefly (only one sentence if possible) tells the reader what the specification covers.

Applicable Documents. The title, number, and date of any document which is referred to elsewhere in the specification are also listed in the applicable document section. These documents are listed under the category of document to which each belongs, such as standards, drawings, specifications, etc.

Requirements. This section is where the exact physical and chemical requirements are given. These may include dimensional, strength, and chemical composition requirements.

Quality Assurance Provisions. The quality assurance section is used to tell the reader how the item is checked to determine if all requirements are met. The step-by-step procedure for this checking must be either written into this section or be included by reference to another document that presents the procedure.

Preparation for Delivery. This section gives the packaging and marking requirements to which the material or item must conform.

Notes. This section may consist of a variety of information which the writer thinks is necessary, such as the intended use of the material or item and ordering data which the procurement document should specify.

Although the vocational writer seldom needs to write a specification requiring all these sections, or to fill in the detail used in the specification format, he may have to use this type of document sometime during his career.

Instructions

Instructions are used to tell the reader how to do something; they have a fairly simple form. The opening sentences usually identify the process and specify any special equipment needed to do the job. The extent of these introductory sentences depends on the complexity of the job. These are followed by the body of the text. The body consists of the major steps in the order that they must be performed to do the job. Fig. 14 shows an example of a short set of instructions for a plumbing job.

EXTENDING THE WATER SUPPLY

Introduction

Extending the water supply may involve anything from adding a faucet to installing a completely new bathroom. The type and number of plumbing tools needed will depend upon the job that is to be done. However, it is best to have all the tools available that might be needed instead of having to find them after the job has been started.

Adding the piping

The first step is to select a starting point. This may be an elbow which can be replaced with a T-fitting. This will provide the connection for the new run of pipe. The pipe ends should be coated with flux before connection is made to the T-fitting. The pipe should be inserted into the fitting and the joint heated until it reaches solder melting temperature. Then flow in the solder to seal the connection.

If the extension of pipe is led through walls, ceilings, or enclosed floors, soft tubing makes the job much simpler and reduces the chances of leaks.

If needed, a valve can be placed somewhere along the line at an accessible point. It can be used to shut off the water flow while work is being completed on the remainder of the job. Such a valve may come in handy for minor repairs in the future.

If the plumbing leads to a room or garage that is being added, the pipe extension should be made before the walls are put up. This is much easier than having to extend it through walls.

Fig. 14. An example of an instructional document.

Descriptive Reports

A descriptive report, as the name suggests, describes how something works. In its introduction the reader is told what the report is about and any general information needed to

AUTO HANDBRAKE

Introduction

This report describes the function of the automobile handbrake. The handbrake lever is located inside the automobile within easy reach of the driver. It may be on the left or the right side of the driver's seat, or under the dashboard.

How the handbrake works

The movement of the handbrake lever is transmitted via a pull rod, a shaft with an arm and pull rod to a clevis. From the clevis the movement is transmitted through cables, as shown, to the rear wheel brake levers. The upper end of these brake levers are attached to the rear brake shoes. When the lever is pulled, the shoes move outward and press against the brake drums, thus applying the handbrake.

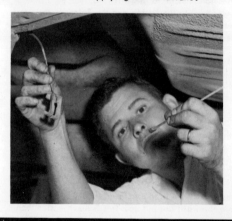

Fig. 15. An example of brief description report.

make the description clear is presented. The body of the report describes how the object works.

Fig. 15 tells how an automobile mechanic might describe the function of the handbrake on an automobile. A somewhat more complex description report is shown in Fig. 16, which describes the disc brake and its method of operation.

THE AUTOMOBILE DISC BRAKE

Introduction

This report describes the function of the automobile disc brake. The brake is applied using the same type of foot pedal used with regular drum brakes. However, the parts and the functioning of the two types of brake systems differ considerably.

The disc are made of steel and are attached to the wheel hubs with which they rotate.

How the disc brake works

On each axle there is a caliper containing the wheel unit cylinders and brake pads. The caliper consists of two halves joined together and located on either side of the brake disc. The brake pads have moulded-in facings and are guided by means of guide pins.

The wheel cylinders are connected to the master cylinders by channels in the caliper housings, connecting lines, and brake lines. As a result of brake application, the pressure rises and the plungers inside the caliper housing move out and press the brake pads against the rotating disc. The pressure of the brake pads, and therefore the braking effect, vary with the pressure applied to the brake pedal.

Fig. 16. An example of a more complex description report.

Progress Reports

Progress reports are used to tell the reader how much work has been done during a certain period of time. Such reports are prepared at regular intervals: daily, weekly, monthly, quarterly, semiannually, or even annually. A series of these reports gives the reader a running account of the work on the project. The series of reports end when the project is completed.

Anyone working on a job that is going to take days, weeks, or months to complete will almost certainly have to give someone a progress report. They are given to those people who need to keep in touch with what is going on. They are used as a means of telling the reader whether the project is on schedule or not, and if not, why it is not. Although progress reports are sometimes given orally, the projects that are long and complex usually require written reports.

As indicated before, the obvious purpose of a progress report is to show what has been done on the particular project. It may also serve as a record for future reference.

Often these reports are used by their readers to decide whether to continue the work, give it new direction or emphasis, or discontinue it. Consequently, it is important that a full account of the progress, or the lack of it, be made clear to the reader.

The form of progress reports depends primarily upon the subject matter and on what the readers want to know. It may be in chronological order. That is, the writer may give the events in the order that they occurred on the job. In some cases it may be better to divide the material by the exact subject matter, such as equipment, materials, personnel and costs. These are the factors vital to the job. It is generally best to use the latter plan unless the report is very brief and covers but a short period of time.

Whether it is straight production work, investigative work, or construction work, someone needs to know how the work is progressing. Although almost any project today must fit into a schedule, there is probably no type of work that is more rigorously controlled by schedule than construction. Therefore, the progress on construction projects is followed closely. Those in construction trades are likely to be directly involved in preparing progress reports for the projects on which they are working. It is because of this frequent involvement that a highway construction project is used as the subject of the example outline shown in Fig. 17. Note that this outline divides the subject into the vital factors of the job. This type of plan is used

HIGHWAY CONSTRUCTION REPORT
PROGRESS REPORT NO. 4
(JULY 19--)

1.   INTRODUCTION
     1.1   Description of project
     1 2   Summary of earlier progress

2.   Details of progress during this period
     2.1   Grading
               2.1.1   Clearing
               2.1.2   Cutting
                         2.1.2.1   Dirt
                         2.1.2.2   Stone
               2.1.3   Fill
                         2.1.3.1   Dirt
                         2.1.3.2   Stone
     2.2   Structures
               2.2.1   Bridges
               2.2.2   Culverts
               2.2.3   Retaining walls
     2.3   Surfacing
               2.3.1   Sub-base
               2.3.2   Pavement
     2.4   Cleanup
               2.4.1   Construction
                         2.4.1.1   Curbs
                         2.4.1.2   Guard rails
               2.4.2   Landscaping
                         2.4.2.1   Finished grading
                         2.4.2.2   Planting

3.   Personnel
     3.1   Personnel requirements to date
     3.2   Future personnel requirements

4.   Costs
     4.1   Costs since last report
     4.2   Total costs to date
     4.3   Future costs

Fig. 17. An example of a progress report outline for a construction project.

Fig. 18. An outline for a simple progress report.

because of the obviously long and complex project that this outline represents.

For those projects that require much less time to complete and are less complex, a simple report form as represented by the outline shown in Fig. 18 might be used by the vocational writer.

On-the-Job Safety Reports

It should not be necessary to repeat in this text the importance of safety on the job. Safety programs are an important aspect of running any type of business today. An organized system of reporting can contribute a great deal to the success of these safety programs. In fact, such a program without some type of reporting is almost doomed.

Somewhat basic to any safety reporting system is the accident report form. This is the report that should start the action that will hopefully prevent such accidents in the future. Perhaps less frequently used in most organizations is the report prepared from records. This type of report is used to point out accident trends and to indicate where emphasis is needed.

Accident Reporting. The record of accidents and the possible reduction of them depends upon the accuracy and completeness of the individual accident reports. The report form must provide for all the essential information; yet it must be as simple as possible so that it is not too much of a burden for an individual to complete. The forms used by industry for this type of report vary widely. Frequently the nature of the business and the environmental factors involved influence the design of the accident report form. The specific information needed on such a report in a chemical plant could be quite different from that needed on a construction site. This is the reason that many firms design their own forms, and sometimes an individual plant designs its own particular form. However, the use of several different forms may result in so many inconsistencies that the particular firm or industry will be unable to use the reports in classifying and compiling accident information. It is therefore better to standardize the form as much as possible. Such a standardized form is represented by the National Safety Council accident report form shown in Fig. 19. Compare this form to that shown in Fig. 20.

Basically, a completed accident report form should:

(1) Provide information that will help determine the cause of the accident

(2) Permit the accident to be classified as to type and location

(3) Provide information that is adequate for insurance carriers and agencies that may investigate the accident —as well as information that will permit a complete analysis so that similar accidents might be prevented in the future

---

ACCIDENT REPORT

Date this report _____

Person reporting _____   Name of injured person _____

Check (for employees only)   ____ patient injury

____ First-aid case, or ____ disabling (lost-time) injury   ____ employee or staff injury

____ On duty, or ____ off duty   ____ visitor injury

Occupation (if employee) _____ _____ Age____ Sex____

Date of injury _____ time _____ a.m. p.m. Place occurred _____

DESCRIPTION OF ACCIDENT

ANSWER FOR ALL CASES

1. What did the injured person DO which caused the accident?_____
_____
_____

2. What other person was involved?_____ What did that person do which contributed to the accident?_____

3. Did defective equipment, furnishings or other unsafe CONDITION contribute to the accident?____ What was wrong?_____
_____

4. What persons other than the injured saw the accident? Identify fully_____
_____

PATIENT CASES ONLY

5. Condition of patient before the accident? (check) disoriented____ senile____ sedated____ normal and alert____ other condition?_____

6. Were bed rails present?____ Were bed rails up?____ down?____

7. What is patient's statement as to causes of accident?_____
_____
_____

Fig. 19. National Safety Council accident report form.

It can be seen that report forms developed at individual plants may appear adequate but are likely to leave out very important information that would make the report almost useless for comparative purposes. The accident records compiled by a single location do not offer evidence as to whether

Ford

EMPLOYEE SERVICE DEPARTMENT

SAFETY SECTION ACCIDENT REPORT

PLANT, DEPOT, ETC. _____ DEPT. NO. _____

NAME OF
INSURED _____ BADGE NO. _____
           FIRST   MIDDLE   LAST

PLACE OF
ACCIDENT _____

DATE OF   TIME OF
INJURY _____ INJURY _____ SHIFT NO. _____

                                       LENGTH OF TIME
JOB CLASSIFICATION _____ ON PRESENT JOB _____

LENGTH OF SERVICE   FORMAN
IN THE COMPANY _____ IN CHARGE _____

HOW THE ACCIDENT HAPPENED:

CHECK ONE OF THE FOLLOWING (FOR PURPOSE OF SAFETY STATICS ONLY)
             INDUSTRIAL ☐   NON–INDUSTRIAL ☐
GIVE THE EXTEND OF KNOWN INJURY:

LIST WITNESSES: (1) NAME _____ BADGE NO. _____
                (2) NAME _____ BADGE NO. _____

IMPORTANT: WHAT ACTION WAS TAKEN FOR PREVENTION OF RECURRENCE ?

DATE OF   SIGNATURE OF
THIS REPORT _____ INVESTIGATOR _____

INSERT CODE

                      UNSAFE MECHANICAL
        AGENCY [_____] OR PHYSICAL CONDITION [_____]

                              UNSAFE
 ACCIDENT TYPE [_____] UNSAFE ACT [_____] PERSONAL FACTOR [_____]

Fig. 20. Ford Motor Co. accident report form. Compare Fig. 19 with Fig. 20.

MINOR ACCIDENT REPORT

Date_____

Location of Accident ________________________

Time of accident _______________

Names of employee(s) involved ____________________

Names of those injured ____________________

Nature of injury ______________________________

Describe how accident happened ____________________

Names of witnesses ______________________________

Classification No. ____________ Prepared by __________

Fig. 21. Minor accident report form.

the accident situation there is normal or completely out of line with other locations.

There may be considerable disagreement as to the necessity of reporting or recording injuries of a minor nature that cause no disability and require no medical attention. But, when viewed from the standpoint of cause and the possibility of future prevention, it becomes clear that even though the accident was minor it cannot be ignored. A minor accident today may be the clue to a serious accident that could happen in the future. A tool knocked from an elevated platform may not cause any harm at all the first time it drops. The next time it could strike and seriously injure someone or possibly cause a death. For this reason many organizations insist that *all* minor accidents as well as major ones be reported. A short form, such as shown in Fig. 21, will often be adequate for minor accidents. Its main advantage is that it requires very little time to fill in and complete.

Reporting From Safety Records. It is not enough just to report accidents and injuries. The information compiled from these reports, as indicated before, is an important aspect of

Fig. 22. Safety equipment in use.

any safety program. It is fundamental in any safety program that all employees be informed about the progress being made in accident prevention and where they stand in comparison to other departments, plants, and industries. The use of face guards, or hard hats as shown in Fig. 22, is an example of how accident reporting and analysis has resulted in development of new safety equipment.

Sometimes this information is reported orally in safety meetings. Often, however, it is also presented in the form of reports to all those concerned. Such reports should not be purely statistical. The writer should also describe what he wants to point out and not just use the numbers that have been gathered.

Reports on the accident prevention program should not be too lengthy. They should be informative but concise. Long reports will not be read by all of those who should read them. These reports should:

(1) Indicate the frequency of accidents
(2) Show the severity of the accidents
(3) Point out the work time lost because of accidents
(4) Show comparisons between departments and plants as well as comparisons between this month and last month, this year and last year.

Care must be exercised by the writer in translating the information that he gathers into language or figures that will be understandable by all the readers. For example, it may be advisable to show the number of man-days worked since the last lost-time accident instead of showing the frequency of accidents by a particular group or department. Also, a brief description of serious accidents that have occurred recently, along with recommendations made for the correction of the causes of these accidents, may be of considerable advantage in these reports.

EXERCISES

1. Prepare an equipment failure report for the last breakdown that you experienced with any type of machinery or vehicle. Decide whether a special form should be used for your report or whether the report requires a form that provides for more narrative explanations.
2. What are the basic differences between memorandum and letter reports?
3. Inspect and write a report describing the building—house or apartment—where you live. Draw conclusions and make recommendations for improvements to the building.
4. What are the three basic letter styles used in modern organizations? What is the most popular style?
5. Write a report on the progress that you have seen during a recent period on a local construction project (highway, street, office building, etc.)

6. Write a report describing the function of a hand tool with which you are familiar. Assume that your reader is completely unfamiliar with the tool.

7. Write a memorandum report to your instructor in which you discuss a project on which you are working in a shop. Describe the progress being made, tell why you are working on this particular project, or describe the proposed use of the object that you are making.

8. Reports to employees on an accident prevention program should cover what four major points?

9. Investigate and prepare a report on the advantages and disadvantages of using at least three different pieces of equipment to do a particular job. If you do not have personal knowledge of each piece of equipment, interview someone who does know about it. Prepare conclusions and recommendations drawn from the facts in the report.

10. Prepare an accident report form that will fit the needs of a particular shop in which you work.

11. What is the purpose of progress reports? What decisions are made from their content?

12. Write a letter report to your instructor using the full block style. The subject chosen in Exercise 6 may be used again or a different subject may be selected.

13. What questions does the investigation report usually answer?

14. Prepare a minor accident report on an accident that has happened recently in your vocational specialty.

15. Name the six sections of a specification. Describe briefly the purpose of each section.

16. Why is it best to standardize accident report forms as much as possible?

17. Prepare a specification sheet for a small object such as a piece of pipe or a tool box which you have in your shop or home.

18. Prepare an oral report on the last accident which happened to you. Your report will be presented in class.

This man is coupling EMT (electrical metallic tubing) from box to box over some flat deck construction which will have a distribution panel in the room below. The slab in which they are to be embedded may be from four to eight inches thick, depending on structural design. One or two levels of reinforced steel bars will support the concrete floor. A progress report will be written by the foreman of this project. (Republic Steel Corporation)

CHAPTER 11

Editing and Proofreading

What's the difference between editing and proofreading? Aren't they both the same thing? Yes, the goal of both is to improve the rough drafts of written communications.

However, editing is usually done on rough drafts before formal proofreading and involves making major changes to the handwritten or typewritten text. Pure proofreading comes later, on the *final* draft, to indicate typographical errors or minor changes which must be made by the typist.

Editing

It would be marvelous if you wrote a perfect draft the first time, but even professional writers can rarely do that. Simple business letters and memoranda can be written perfectly the first time—with practice. But technical reports, manuals, specifications, proposals, and other documents usually require at least one editing. Sometimes several editings are needed until good judgment tells you to quit!

There is a great deal of difference between trying to edit your own work and that of someone else. It is usually easier to see mistakes in the writing of someone else than in your own. Somehow a psychological phenomenon called "pride of authorship" prevents us from seeing our own writing faults.

In most employment situations, you will not have a professional editor handy to assist you with your work. Usually you must complete the document alone—with only clerical aid in the typing phase.

Just how can you editorially attack a rough draft document and give it the necessary polish in an objective way?

It is valuable (but not essential) to use the proofreading symbols shown in Figs. 1, 2, and 3 when indicating editorial changes. Use of these symbols will avoid a great deal of oral explanation to typists who will make the necessary changes. Proofreading symbols save time.

If you have a rough draft to edit, use this checklist to ensure that you have a quality document:

(1) First read the document to get a general concept of its weaknesses.

(2) Next, check the outline for consistency. Make certain that you don't have an A without a B or a 1 without a 2, etc. Make certain that all text material under a particular sideheading is a discussion of the subject indicated by that sideheading.

(3) Cross out any unnecessary paragraphs and sentences. It takes courage to delete *that* paragraph which is most interesting to you but which has no relevant part in the written discussion. Remove it anyway!

(4) Rearrange the order of those paragraphs and sentences which are not in a logical sequence. Often, material can be rearranged by cutting a page into parts and reassembling sentences and paragraphs with transparent tape.[1]

(5) Rewrite those paragraphs and sentences which are awkward, too long, too short, or really don't say what you want to report.

[1]Transparent tape is recommended for this purpose because it can be written on with ink or lead pencil. It is manufactured by several leading firms.

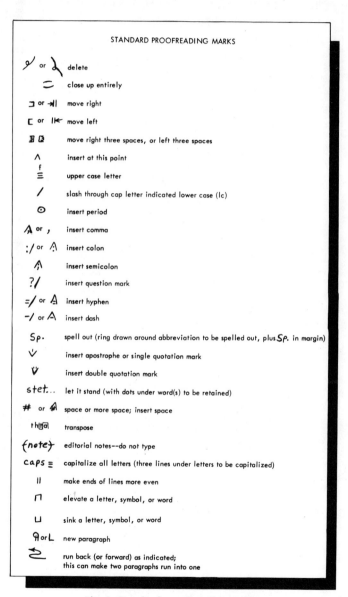

Fig. 1. Standard proofreading marks.

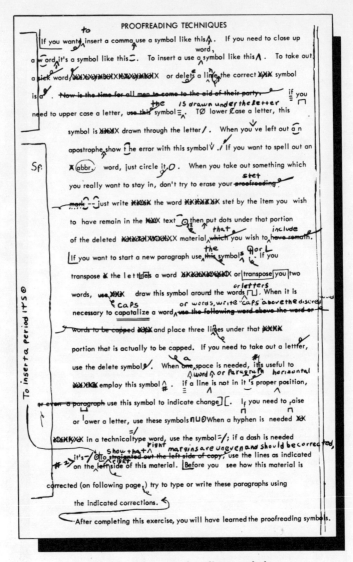

Fig. 2. Using proofreading symbols.

(6) Reread the document and correct the grammar, punctuation, capitalization, typographical and spelling errors.

Your rough draft should be ready for a second typing. Repeat the above six steps on further drafts, if necessary.

PROOFREADING TECHNIQUES (CONT)

If you want to insert a comma, use a symbol like this⋀ . If you need to close up a word, it's a symbol like this⊂ . To insert a word, use a symbol like this⋀ . To take out a word or delete a line, the correct symbol is a ℰ. If you need to upper case a letter, the symbol ☰ is drawn under the letter. To lower case a letter, this symbol is drawn through the letter / . When you've left out an apostrophe, show the error with this symbol ⋁. If you want to spell out an abbreviation, circle it ◯ and mark S ρ. When you take out something which you really want to stay in, don't try to erase your proofreading mark--just write the word "stet" by the item you wish to have remain in the text. Then, put dots under that portion of the deleted material that you wish to include.

If you want to start a new paragraph, use the symbols ⁋ or ∟. If you transpose the letters in a word or you transpose two words, draw this symbol around the words or letters ∏⌐ . When it is necessary to CAPITALIZE a word or words, write "caps" above the desired word and place three lines under that portion that is actually to be capped. If you need to take out a letter, use the delete symbol ℰ. When a space is needed, it is useful to employ this symbol ⌃#. If a line, word, or paragraph is not in its proper horizontal position, use this symbol to indicate change ⊐⊏. If you need to raise a letter or lower a letter, use these symbols ∏⌐. When a hyphen is needed in a technical-type word, use the symbol =/; if a dash is needed, it's –/. To insert a period it's ⊙ .

To show that right margins are uneven and should be corrected, use the lines as indicated on the right side of this material.

Before you see how this material is corrected (on following page) try to type or write these paragraphs using the indicated corrections. After completing this exercise, you will have learned the proofreading symbols.

Fig. 3. Retyped material where typist made the corrections indicated by following editor's proofreading symbols.

Figs. 4, 5 and 6 indicate several steps in the editorial process where proofreading symbols have been used to improve a memorandum.

A meeting will be held at Allen Jones Steel Company to discuss three new company inventions and their development and production and market potenial and technical improvements th.1t these inventions have made pos- sible The meeting will be held at 3:30 p.m. and the stainless steel retain- ing rod; the electronic computer erase; and the new cold-steel rolling device will be the main topic under discussion. All presons attending the meeting should come to the conference room of the Engineering Laboratory Building

The meeting will held to determine what technical information should be included in the company's report to stockholders about research prog- ress and to gove such information to the advertising and public relations presonnel who will be in attendance. The meeting will be conducted in four parts; (1) a brief talk by Mr. John M. Supervisor; (2) a brief talk by Mr. F. R. Advertising Manager; (3) a roung-table discussion by the group; and (4) presentations of reports by each member of the group on his specialty connected with the three inventions. The meeting will be held Monday, April 4.

Fig. 4. Rough draft of a memorandum.

Proofreading

You have your final draft typed, and you're ready to proof- read the copy. The primary task here is to ensure that the typist has performed properly. You are making a quality

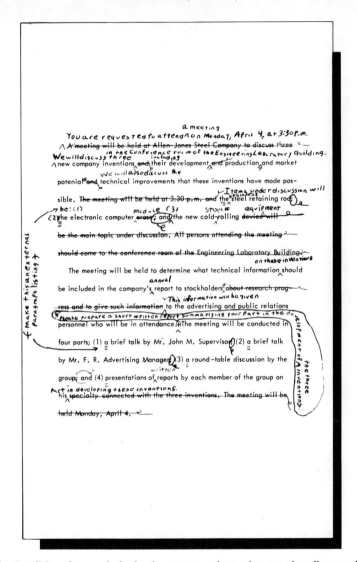

Fig. 5. Editing the rough draft of a memorandum using proofreading symbols.

control check of the typing. In proofreading, you may find additional errors which you somehow missed earlier. The following procedures are a part of proofing the final draft:

MEMORANDUM

To: Distribution

From: John M. Supervisor

Date: April 20, 19--

Subject: Meeting to Discuss New Inventions

You are requested to attend a meeting on Monday, April 4, at 3:30 p.m in the conference room of the Engineering Laboratory Building. We will discuss three new company inventions, including their development, production, and market potential. We will also discuss the technical improvements that these inventions have made possible.

Items under discussion will be:

(1) The stainless steel retaining rod

(2) The elctronic computer module

(3) The new cold steel rolling device

The meeting will be held to determine what technical information on these inventions should be included in the company's annual report to stockholders. This information will be given to the advertising and public relations personnel who will be in attendance.

Please prepare a short written report summarizing your part in the development of the three inventions.

The meeting will be conducted in four parts:

(1) A brief talk by Mr John M. Supervisor

(2) A brief talk by Mr. F. R. Advertising Manager

Fig. 6. Corrected and retyped memorandum.

(1) Inspect each page to ensure a neat appearance, that corrections have been properly made, and that no smudges remain. Make certain that headings and text have the proper spacing and that material is not too close to edges of the paper.

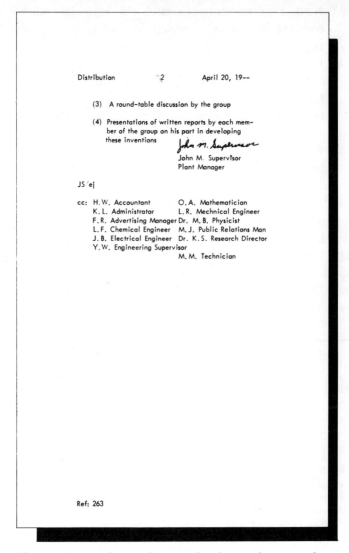

Distribution   -2   April 20, 19--

(3) A round-table discussion by the group

(4) Presentations of written reports by each member of the group on his part in developing these inventions

John M. Supervisor

John M. Supervisor
Plant Manager

JS/ej

cc: H.W. Accountant   O.A. Mathematician
     K.L. Administrator   L.R. Mechnical Engineer
     F.R. Advertising Manager Dr. M.B. Physicist
     L.F. Chemical Engineer   M.J. Public Relations Man
     J.B. Electrical Engineer   Dr. K.S. Research Director
     Y.W. Engineering Supervisor
                        M.M. Technician

Ref: 263

Fig. 6 (cont). Second page of corrected and retyped memorandum.

(2) Examine each page to ensure that everything which should be on that page is there. For example, a business letter could need an "Enc.: As stated" line which had been forgotten.

(3) Next, read carefully through the material, noting any corrections lightly in pencil. Use of proofreading symbols is not essential but they help.

(4) Finally, set your rough draft and final draft side by side in front of you. Using the index finger on each hand, make a word by word comparison between the two drafts. If you're uncertain about the spelling of a word, look it up in your dictionary.

(5) After the typist has completed the corrections, check them to ensure that all have been properly made.

Just how accurate should a document be? Theoretically all errors should be eliminated, but we know from experience that it is almost impossible to turn out page after page of perfectly written and typed work under ordinary business circumstances. One typographical, punctuation, or grammatical error in each five pages of work is excellent. One or two errors per page is no good!

EXERCISES

1. Edit the following letter, looking for all types of errors:

Allen-Jones Steel Co.
Steel Road
Chicago, Illinoi 12765
January 20, 19—

Salco Electronics, Inc
261 South Sandpit Street
Ithaca, New York 12131
Attension: Mr. M. M. Seller
Subject: Contract Award, Electron Tube

You may be interesting to learn that through testing of your sample tubes was conducted by Allen-Jones Steel Company Quality control Laboratory.

The results of this testing showed that you have a superior electron tube which is relative efficient and has adequate life.

Needless to say, we have enclosed a contract for your approval.

This contract lists the exact and the precise specifications for the manufacture of the electron tubes in cluding the materials of fabrication. The specifications are based upon an

examination of the sample tubes you gave us and the proposal
which you submited with your bid.

We are very, very greatly pleased to award salco Electronics,
Inc., Ithaca New York, a contract for the manufacture of 1000
Model S123 electron tubes. Your firm was the lowest bider in the
field of four competing firms for the production of these tubes at
$10.27 dollars per each and every unit. Competing firms were
(1) Aymes Manufacturing Company; (2) Smith tool Company,
the Electronic Corporation of America and Salco Electrical.
Thus, we have enclosed the contract. Would you please examine
the enclosed contract and return it signed. If you have any
question, please phone me at once. Mr. R. V. Jones, President of
Alen-Jones Steel Co. has signed the contract for our part of
the agrement. Wewill expect to receive the signedcopy no later
than March 1 19—.

Best wishes for your efforts to meed the delivery schedule
for the tubes on time; we will expect to receive the first shipment
of 100 tubes on April 15, 19—. It is the policy of Alen-Jones
Co. not to reveal the results of competitivebidding None of the
biding competitors will learn of your price, you may rest assured.

Very truly yours
Allen-JONES STEEL COMPANY
Chicago, ILLINOIS
R. N. BAGGS
Comptreller

RB/ss

2. Edit and rewrite, if necessary, the following procedure.
Make two drawings which show the procedural steps or the
components. Include these drawings as Figs. 1 and 2.

PROCEDURE TO UNCRATE PRESSURE CHAMBER
(FOLLOWING SHIPMENT)

Procedure

This document describes the procedures used in the uncrating
and the inspecting the condition of the chambers when received
from the vendor, prior to the installation.

Uncrating style

Equipment includes—one container, reusable (crate) (no.
31B); 2 crate retaining clamps and straps (inside of case, used
to hold chamber in place in case), chamber is a cylinder, 2 ft. in
dia.×6 feet long, and 1 inch thick. Temperuture Recorder
inside case, mounted on end, w/3 phillips screws. Open-end
wrench, ¾ opening on one end and ⅝ opening on other end.
Transpost Dolly. 1 medium Phillips screwdriver. (See Figures
1 and 2)

Uncrating Procedure

(1) Using ¾ open-end wrench, remove ends and sides of crate

(2) Remove top of crate. Be very very careful when taking crate apart not to let the tops, ends or sides fall on the chamber

(3) Before removing the top and sides look for temperature recorder on inside of right end of case. If the recorder has exceeded 97° F, do not continue with uncrating, because case may be heat damaged It is then removed from case, using phillips screwdriver.

(4) All uncrating procedures shall be accomplished in a room that is temperature controlled at 70° ±5 deg. f., and this room temperature shall be continuously recorded, with a recorder separate from the one in the crate which was used to record temperatures during shipment.

(5) Then, remove retaining clamps and retaining straps, by taking off wing nuts. Case is then setting loose in 2 cushioned plywood "U" frames, attached to the base of the case.

(6) Inspect, thoroughly, all exterior and interior surfaces of the chamber for damage. Take close-up polorid photographs of any damage! Report any damage at once to the Department Manager. Also, after ends of crate have been removed, inspect for damage then before removing sides and top.

(7) The chamber is then ready for formal quality control testing and inspection. Place chamber on transport dolly and roll (carefully) to quality control department.

Conclusions

The chamber is a delicate unit, requiring great care in handling, uncrating, etc. Be careful with it. It is made from a filiment wound fiberglass structure.

3. Edit this company research capabilities summary:

SALECO, INC.
RESEARCH AND DEVELOPMENT CAPABILITIES

Saleco maintains an organization of technically competent personnal, to perform research and development contracts, for instrumentation needs.

Our capability's include graduate engineers, scientists, and technicians who are fabulous specialists in advanced solid state electronics, microcircuits, nuclear measuring instruments, transducers, sensing devices, liquid metal instrumation, computor components and telemetry. Saleco stays abreast of advanced control technology such as digital computors which is gaining ground in the electrical utility industry. Saleco has brought together a highly competent electrical contracting capability, with industrial computer control specialists Let Saleco perform as consultants on your computor control program, or take full responsibility for design of the control system and assembly of the computer equipment.

Our engineers are fuly conversent on a wide range of computer compounds

Saleco's R & D capability includes among other things, a fine tradition in the performance of engineering study contracts. Saleco performed an exciting engineering study to determine the feasibility of employing a instrumentation and control system for nuclear power plants, including, boiling H_2O, pressurized water, liquid metal, gas cooling of reactor.

Saleco has capacity for printing (publishing) research & development reports, specifications, manuals, and other tech documentation this capability includes a thoroughly effective knowledge of techniques for preparing deocuments according to strict Govt. specs. Salecos developmental lab is equiped with a wide range of electronic test equipment. The lab may perform environmental test chamber tests with elevated temp humidity, & reliability tests. Can also do tests on tinsil strength tests, shock & vibration, cryogenic tests, radiographic tests.

4. Edit this report on construction work for a facility to remove SO_2 and particulates from coal-burning electrical generating plant flue gasses. Make a bar graph showing construction progress. Make a table showing test results on the particulate portion of the plant, and another table showing the environmental control standards,[1] instead of presenting them in paragraph form.

CONSTRUCTION REPORT
FACILITY TO REMOVE PARTICULATES AND SO_2
FROM
ELECTRICAL GENERATING PLANT
FLUE GASS

I. *Introduction*

This facility is being built by Garguantua Construction Co. at the Edison Electric Company, Tuson, Arizona, to meet federal government and state air pollution standards. Those standards include for suspended particulate: $70\mu g/m^3$ - maximum anual geometric mean; $100\mu g/m^3$ - maximum 24-hour arithmetic mean.

---

[1]These standards are only approximate, and are *not* presented in this book as *actual* standards.

For ambient sulfur dioxide (SO₂) :0.0/8 ppm - maximum annual average; .088 ppm - maximum 24-hr average; .30 parts per million maximum 1-hr. average. 0.042 parts/million - maximum any 3 consecutive days. Measurements to be taken 1,000 ft. from power plant stack

Rate of particulate emission when coal burned is: when 1000 lb/hr of coal is burned, 2.58 lb/hr of particulate can be emitted from stack. 2,000 lb/hr, 4.1 lb/hr; 4000 lb/hr—6.52 lb/hr. 10,000 lb/hr—12.0 lb/hr, 20,000 lb/hr.) 19.2 lb/h4. 50,000 lb/hr, 35.4 lb/hr; 100,000 lb/hr, 44.6 lb/hr. Measurements to be taken by stack monitors.

The Edison Electric generating plant burns 50,000 lbs per hour, coal. The entire particulate removal system is now installed (as of April 20) and has been successfully tested. The unit consists of 3 electrostatic precipitators, in line. Cost is $1,000,350,27. dollars. Scheduled completion date for precipitator installation was April 1, 19—. Dust is removed from the precipitators and bagged, to prevent blowing. The precipitators were mounted on concrete footings and concrete pillars.

Stack monitor tests show that the particulate going through the stack is below that permitted:

April	26	9-10 am	40.6 lb/hr
	27	10-11 am	39.2 lb/hr
	28	1- 2 am	40.1 lb./hr
	29	1- 2 pm	instr. failure
	30	1- 2 pm	40.6
	31	3- 4 pm	40.9
May	1	1- 2 am	41.3
	2	1- 2 pm	43.6
	3	2 -3 pm	41.4
	4	2- 3 am	41.4
	5	10-11 pm	42.2
	6	10-11 am	43.0

Ambient monitoring 1,000 feet from the stack, however, shows results which do not meet standards setting a maximum 24-hour arithmetic mean:

April	26	101	$\mu g/m^3$
	27	105	$\mu g/m^3$
	28	107	$\mu g/m^3$
	29	106	$\mu g/m^3$
	30	103	$\mu g/m^3$
May	1	113	$\mu g/m^3$
	2	103	$\mu g/m^3$
	3	104	$\mu g/m^3$

4   101 $\mu g/m^3$
5   103 $\mu g/m^3$
6   115 $\mu g/m^3$

We think the ambient standards are high because this is a heavily populated industrial district with several stacks around the area.

Construction of the over-all plant for SO_2 removal is now 50 percent complete; this plant is consisting of 3 in-line scrubbers being built after the electrostatic precipitation equipment and, of course before the stack. Individual construction phases are at this level: concrete footings, 100% complete; concrete pillars, 100 percent complete; steel erection, 100 per cent complete; scrubbers are set in place and installation is 50% complete. Piping is 10 percent complete; Electrical is 10% complete.

We expect installation and final construction to be complete by January 1, 19—. We are presently on schedule.

Conclusions

The electrostatic precipitators have been tested with both good and bad results. See Table I. The electrostatic precipitator portion of the facility is now complete. The SO_2 portion is now under construction and is approximately 50 percent complete. (See Fig. 1.)

Later, the facility for generating power must be closed down to hook up the scrubbers to the cleaning chain between the furnace-boiler complex and the stack, just as was done when the precipitators were installed.

Review of Grammar

Grammar is the study of all those rules that treat the construction, form and usage of words.

Eight Basic Parts of Speech

The eight basic parts of speech are:

(1) Noun
(2) Pronoun
(3) Verb
(4) Adverb
(5) Adjective
(6) Preposition
(7) Conjunction
(8) Interjection

A short form definition of these basic parts of speech include:

(1) Naming words—{ Nouns / Pronouns

(2) Action words—{ Verbs

(3) Descriptive words—{ Adjectives / Adverbs

(4) Connective words—{ Conjunctions / Prepositions

(5) Expressing emotion—{ Interjections

Nouns. A *noun* is a word that names something:

person	Mr. W. R. Apser
place	New York City
thing	rock
quality	love
concept	construction, democracy

There are two general classifications of nouns:

(1) *Common noun*—the name of a general group or class, not capitalized:

dog, horse, man, day, park, honesty, courtesy, happiness

(2) *Proper noun*—the name of someone or something specific, always capitalized:

Lyman, Nancy, Mr. W. E. Day, the Arctic, Bear River, Los Angeles, Washington Monument, League of Women Voters, Empire State Building, American Technical Society, International Business Machines, Inc.

Another way of classifying nouns:

(1) *Collective nouns*—name a group:

dogs, man, IBM Corporation, cattle, Catholic Church, men

(2) *Abstract nouns*—name an abstract thing:

beauty, love, happiness, socialism, death

(3) *Concrete nouns*—name specific physical items:

house, rock, steel, copper, tree, pipe, gas, automobile, baby, man, woman, money

In a sentence, a noun is used in four basic ways:

(1) As a subject of the sentence:

This *carburetor* is out of adjustment.

(2) As an object of a sentence:

He will clean the *carburetor*.

(3) As an object of a preposition:

Set the idle screw on the *carburetor*.

(4) As a subjective complement—renaming the subject:

The welder was a *lady*.

Pronouns. A *pronoun* is a word used in place of a noun or as a substitute for a noun. There are nine types:

(1) *Personal:* I, you, he, she, it, we, they, me, him, her, us, them.

Indicates person(s) speaking:

I believe it is right.

Indicates person(s) spoken to:

Are *you* going?

Indicates person(s) or things spoken of:

She is making the test.

(2) *Demonstrative:* this, that, these, those.

Indicates a person or thing already mentioned:

> *Those* people will be assigned.
> *This* means that the damaged parts will be replaced.

(3) *Relative:* who, which, that, what, whoever, whatever, whom.

Indicates reference to a previous noun or pronoun:

> The bolts *that* were sheared weakened the entire structure.
> The fabricator *who* installed those bolts was at fault.

(4) *Interrogative:* who, which, what, whom.

Asks a question:

> *Who* did it?
> *Which* fabricator is responsible?

(5) *Indefinite:* any, anyone, some, someone, somebody, something, nobody.

Indicates indefinite person or thing:

> *Something* (other than structural failure) was suspected as being the cause.

(6) *Intensive or reflexive:* myself, yourself, ourselves, themselves, itself.

Reflexive relates to subject:

> Bowling is *itself* a good exercise.
> I installed the bolts *myself*.

Intensive gives emphasis:

> I *myself* am not satisfied.

(7) *Possessive:* mine, ours, yours, his, hers, theirs, its, one's, somebody's, someone's.

Indicates possession:

> It is *mine*.
> *Someone's* life could be at stake if the structure fails.

(8) *Reciprocal:* one another, each other.

Indicates that each is affected:

> They hit *one another* or *each other*.

(9) *Acting as adjective:* my, its, his, her, one, someone's, their, somebody's, someone's.

> *His* machine was improperly maintained.

Verbs. A *verb* is a word that expresses action, existence or occurrence.

Action:

He *tightened* the oil pan bolts.

Existence:

He *found* water in the crankcase.

Occurrence:

The head gasket *had blown,* permitting water from the cooling system to enter the crankcase.

The main verb is often assisted by auxiliary verbs: can, must, have, had, shall, should, would, could, do, may.

The mechanic *had* seen it happen before.

He *could have been* repairing it.

Verbs are also classified as transitive and intransitive.

A *transitive verb* has a direct object, a direct receiver of the action:

Direct
object

He struck the engine.

An *intransitive verb* does not have a direct object, but instead has a complement which completes the meaning of the verb.

Subjective
complement

The engine *was* still warm.

He *ran.* (no object or complement)

Adjective. An *adjective* is a word that describes or modifies a noun or a pronoun. There are five general forms:

(1) *Descriptive:* pretty, tall, narrow, large.

It is a *dirty* engine.

(2) *Possessive nouns and pronouns:* your, his, mine, its, mother's, John's.

modifies
set

Someone took *his* socket set.

It was found in *John's* tool box.

(3) *Numbers:* one, sixty, etc.

modifies
strut

One strut was spot welded.

(4) *The articles:* a, an, and the.

> *The* structure was weak.
> A man stood too close.
> *An* accident happened.

A is used prior to a word which begins with a consonant. *An* is used prior to a word which begins with a vowel or has a vowel sound:

> A house, but *an* hour

(5) *Indefinites:* each, every, some, several.

> *Several* men will be required.

(6) *Acting as subjective complement:*

modifies
truss

> This truss is *short*.

Adverbs. An *adverb* is a word that modifies a verb, an adjective, another adverb, or the sense of a clause.

Modifying a verb:

modifies
works

> He works *quickly*.

Modifying an adjective:

modifies
significant

> He completed a *highly* significant task.

Modifying another adverb:

modifies
quickly

> He works *very* quickly.

Modifying sense of a clause (*or sentence*):

> *Yes*, it is a condition.
> *Certainly*, the task will be difficult.

There are seven adverbial forms which indicate:

(1) *Place*

modifies
fell

> The structure fell *there*.

(2) *Time*

modifies
happened

This incident happened *yesterday*.

(3) *Manner or quality*

modifies
works

He works *quickly*.

(4) *Direction*

modifies
turn

Turn the nut *counterclockwise*.

(5) *Degree*

modifies
tight

The lug nuts are *very* tight.

(6) *Frequency*

modifies
replaced

The muffler was replaced *twice*.

(7) *Affirmation or negation*

modifies
available

He is *not* available.

modifies sense
of clause

Yes, it is a condition.

Prepositions. A *preposition* is a term that introduces a phrase and shows a relationship between its object and some other word in the sentence. There are two forms:

(1) *Single words:*

about	behind	during	on	till
above	below	for	out	to
across	beneath	from	outside	under
after	between	in	over	until
against	beyond	into	past	up
at	by	of	since	upon
before	down	off	through	with

prepositional
phrase

The structure was attached *to* the footings.

(2) *Two or more words:*

according to	by reason of	in spite of
as for	by way of	instead of
as to	for the sake of	on account of
because of	in keeping with	out of
by means of	in regard to	with respect to

prepositional phrase

The structure collapsed *because of* a weak strut weld.

Conjunctions. A *conjunction* is a word that joins words, phrases or clauses. There are two types:

(1) *Coordinating conjunction:* joins elements of equal rank.

and	but	for
or	yet	nor

Joining two nouns:

The accountant *and* the auditor made their survey.

Joining two verbs:

The accountant compiled *and* added the debits.

Joining two clauses:

Should automobiles have front wheel steering only *or* should back wheels also be designed to turn?

(2) *Subordinating conjunction:* introduces dependent clauses.

after	although	before
until	while	unless

Metal-to-metal contact caused the fire, *after* the lubricant failed.

Interjections. An *interjection* is a word that expresses sudden or strong feeling. It is rarely used in vocational writing.

Help!

Oh, I slipped.

Verbals

Verbals are words which are formed from verbs, but which are used as other parts of speech. Classifications include: gerund, participle and infinitive.

Gerunds. A *gerund* is a verbal used in a sentence as a noun. It must have an —ing ending.

    sentence
    subject

Driving an automobile requires adequate training.

Participles. A *participle* is a verbal used in a sentence as an adjective.

    modifies
     he

Picking up his tools, he left the job.

        modifies
        structure

They examined the *shattered* structure.

        modifies
        girder

We saw a girder *being loaded* onto a truck.

    modifies
    uniform

He removed his *torn* uniform.

    modifies
     man

The *laughing* man turned on the ignition.

Infinitives. An *infinitive* is a verbal used as a noun, an adjective, or an adverb. It consists of the root verb preceded by the word *to*. The word *to* may occasionally be omitted.)

        noun
    (direct object)

Our employees like *to work* the swing shift.

noun
sentence subject

To work the swing shift is easier.

adverb modifying
difficult

A good paragraph is not difficult *to write*.

to
left out

He helped me *tighten* the engine mounts.

to
left out

We could do nothing except *wait*.

It is now proper to split the infinitive by placing an adverb between "to" and the verb, particularly when it makes the sentence less awkward.

No infinitive split:

> The test failed *seriously* to affect the award of the contract.

Split infinitive:

> The test failed to *seriously* affect the award of the contract.

Phrases

A *phrase* is a group of two or more related words not containing a subject *and* a verb. A phrase serves in the sentence as a single part of speech. There are five types considered here: prepositional, participial, absolute, gerund, and infinitive.

(1) *Prepositional*—consists of a preposition, its object, and any modifiers the object may have. Prepositional phrases may be used in a sentence in three ways: as an adjective, an adverb, or a noun.

   (a) *Adjective*

   adjective
   modifies door

   The door *on the car* is frozen shut.

   (b) *Adverb*

   adverb
   modifies ran

   The men ran *into trouble*.

(c) *Noun*

sentence subject

Before lunch is the best time to clean the vat.

(2) *Participial Phrase*—consists of a participle plus any complements or modifiers; acts as adjective in a sentence.

phrase
modifies plumber

The plumber *installing that water closet* is a journeyman.

(3) *Absolute Phrase*—a special kind of participial phrase which does not have any grammatical relation to the rest of a sentence.

absolute phrase, no grammatical relation

The roof truss being installed off center, we decided to rip it out. (awkward but correct)

(4) *Gerund Phrase*—consists of a gerund plus any complements or modifiers; acts as a noun in a sentence.

noun
subject of sentence

Getting the glass installed caused serious delays.

noun
direct object

I like *working a job for union scale.*

noun
object of preposition upon

Upon *completing the painting*, we will sign the lien waver.

(5) *Infinitive Phrase*—consists of an infinitive plus any complements or modifiers. It may be used in a sentence as an adjective, adverb, or noun.

adjective
modifies job

I wish I had a job *to do today.*

adverb
modifies pleased

I was pleased *to see him.*

noun
subject of sentence

Where to begin was a difficult problem.

noun
object of preposition except

He could do nothing except *resign gracefully*.

noun
direct object

The foreman promised *to do us a favor*.

An infinitive phrase may have a subject but will not stand
alone.

subject
of phrase

We wanted *him to be our supervisor*.

Clauses

A *clause* is a group of related words containing a subject
and a verb. The two types include the independent and dependent forms.

Independent Clause. The *independent clause* will stand alone
as a complete sentence.

subject   verb

A poor workman fights with his tools.

Dependent Clause. The *dependent clause* will not stand alone,
even though it contains a subject and a verb.

subject   verb

That he   drives . . .

subject   verb

Since Mr. Evans started . . .

There are three general types of dependent clauses: adjective, adverbial, and noun. Each begins with a subordinating
conjunction.

conjunction

He purchased one of those houses *that have just been built*.
(adjective clause modifies *houses*)

conjunction

He resigned *because there was too much overtime work.*
(adverbial clause modifies *resigned*)

conjunction

Whether he resigns or not is of no importance to me.
(noun clause acting as subject of sentence)

Sometimes a subordinating conjunction in a dependent clause is left out.

that
left out

I wish *I had a job today.*

The Sentence

A *sentence* is a group of words expressing a complete thought. It must contain a subject and a verb but may also include a direct object, an indirect object, or a subjective complement. Of course the subject, verb and object, or complement can have proper modifiers.

In English, thoughts are normally expressed in sentences which have the sentence elements in a one-two-three left-to-right position. That is, the subject is in position one, the verb in position two, and the object or complement is in position three.

subject verb complement

The electrical outlets are dead.
(1) (2) (3)

However, a few sentences are written in other than left-to-right sequences, particularly when the words here, where, and there begin the sentence.

verb subject

There are 10 damaged cabinets.
(2) (1)

direct
object verb subject verb

Whom did you tell?

Subject Forms. The subject of a sentence must be one of these elements:

Noun	*Jim* welds.
Pronoun	*They* weld.
Gerund	*Welding* requires skill.
Infinitive	*To weld* requires skill.
Gerund phrase	*Welding two sheets* requires skill.
Infinitive phrase	*To weld two sheets* requires skill.
Prepositional phrase	*Before welding* is the time to scrape the surfaces.
Noun clause	*Whoever welded it* must have had training.

One of the most common vocational writing faults concerning subject use is the vague pronoun reference.

> Damage can occur to the AC power unit when the cover is kept closed. *It* has great sensitivity to heat conditions above 200° F. (*It* could refer to *AC power* or to *cover*.)

To clarify:

> Damage can occur to the AC power unit when the cover is kept closed. *The AC unit* has great sensitivity to heat conditions above 200° F. (By repeating the subject there is no question about what has *great sensitivity*.)

Verb Forms. There are six verb tenses that relate to time that events occur. All are appropriate in vocational writing when correctly applied to the individual situation. The verb tenses are:

Present:	I walk. I am walking.
Past:	I walked. I was walking.
Future:	I shall or will walk. I shall or will be walking.
Present perfect:	I have walked. I have been walking.
Past perfect:	I had walked. I had been walking.
Future perfect:	I will or shall have been walking.

Normally, proposals and specifications are written in future tense, instructions in future and/or present tense, and reports in past tense.

Object and Complement Forms. Some sentences stand alone with only a subject and a verb and perhaps some modifiers.

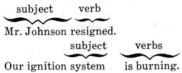

subject   verb

Mr. Johnson resigned.

subject   verbs

Our ignition system   is burning.

Others require something besides the subject and verb to be complete.

subject verb

He enjoys . . .

verb subject verb

Have you tried . . .

Objects and *complements* are words that are added to a subject and a verb to *complete* the meaning.

The *direct object* names the receiver of the transitive verb action.

transitive direct
verb   object

We painted the car.

The *indirect object* names, without the use of a preposition, the person or thing for whom or to which something is done. An indirect object must also have a direct object in the same sentence.

indirect direct
verb object object

He gave me a hammer.

A *subjective complement* may be a noun or pronoun, if it renames the subject, or an adjective if it describes the subject.

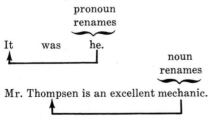

pronoun
renames

It   was   he.

noun
renames

Mr. Thompsen is an excellent mechanic.

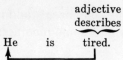

He   is   tired.

An *objective complement* renames or describes the direct object instead of the subject.

They made him president.   I consider him reliable.

Subject-Verb Agreement. Another of the most common faults in written vocational communication is subject-verb agreement. This fault is frequent because people tend to write too fast and there are many verb choices to be made—thus there are many chances for error.

The rule is: Plural and compound subjects (joined by *and*) must have plural verbs; singular subjects must have singular verbs.

Some of the places where error occurs include:

(1) Situations where a prepositional phrase with a plural object occurs between subject and verb. The verb should be singular.

singular subject and verb

> The can of miscellaneous nuts and bolts *is* located in the first drawer.

(2) Situations where verbs *doesn't* and *don't* are used. *Doesn't* is proper with singular subjects; *don't* is used only with plural subjects.

> The operator *doesn't* hear you.
> The operators *don't* hear you.

(3) Situations involving the use of indefinite pronouns, *some, all,* and *most* as sentence subjects. These pronouns are singular when they refer to a quantity, but plural when they refer to a number.

> Some of the work *is* completed. (quantity)
> Some of the tools *are* here. (number)
> All of the bond paper *has* arrived. (quantity)
> All of the problems *have* complications. (number)

(4) Situations involving any and none. These indefinite pronouns follow the same rule as above for number and quantity, but may also be singular or plural, depending on whether the writer is thinking of one thing or several things.

> Any of these tools *is* helpful. (any one)
> Any of these tools *are* helpful. (any tools)

(5) Situations where compound subjects are joined by *and, or, nor, either-or,* or *neither-nor.*

An *and* subject compounding is always plural in verb form except when the *and* is part of a name that is considered singular.

> Mr. Evans and Mr. Smith *are* the drywall contractors.
> Evans and Smith Company *is* the drywall contractor.
> (Notice that the subjective complement noun contractor(s) which renames the subject must also agree.)

Or, nor, either-or, or *neither-nor* subject compounding is always singular in verb form when the final subject is singular.

> Either a box wrench or an open-end wrench *is* needed.

but

> Either a crescent wrench or open-end wrenches *are* needed.

(6) Situations where collective nouns (such as group, crowd, crew) are used. When the writer refers to a group acting as a unit, the subject should be thought of as singular and take a singular verb.

> The design group *is* responsible. (whole group)

When the writer is talking about individual members of the group the verb should be plural.

> The crew *are* taking turns. (one by one)

Person

There are three *person forms* in writing—based upon the various pronoun forms:

First person:
> *I* did ...

Second person:
> *You* did ...

Third person:
  It did . . .

Pronoun forms include:

SINGULAR PERSON

First	*Second*	*Third*		
I	you	he	she	it
my	your	his	her	its
mine	yours	hers	him	
me				

PLURAL PERSON

First	*Second*	*Third*
we	you	they
our	your	their
ours	yours	theirs
us		them

The third person impersonal tone is normally employed for vocational report writing. Sometimes the *we* first person plural is used in place of the first person *I* to avoid the egotistical sound of *I*. However, in writing plans or instructions, the second person form *you* is valuable.

  You should . . .
  You will . . .

Punctuation

Punctuation is a group of marks and symbols that is used in sentence construction to make the words more meaningful. Punctuation should be applied only when it can be used to avoid confusion and put the true meaning of words into the reader's mind.

The 13 standard marks of punctuation are:

(1) The period
(2) The comma
(3) The semicolon
(4) The colon
(5) The question mark
(6) The exclamation point
(7) The apostrophe
(8) The parenthesis
(9) The single quotation mark (rarely used)
(10) The double quotation mark
(11) The hyphen
(12) The dash
(13) The ellipsis

The Period

(1) A period is placed after every sentence that is not an exclamation or a question.

Set the proper gap on this spark plug.

(2) The period is used in some abbreviations. (See Chapter 4.)

a.m.	in.
p.m.	gal.
U.S. Government	No.
New York City, N.Y.	i.e.

However, modern vocational writing usage is to drop periods after all frequently used abbreviations in a technical manuscript.

Some examples are:

ft	Å (angstroms)	cc
psi	°F	yd
ft-lb	°C	sec
mm	ml	min
lb	lb-ft	

(3) The period is used to separate whole numbers from fractions when the decimal system is employed.

1.25 sec	3.5 percent
$12.50	0.25 in.

(4) Use the period inside a parenthesis when an entire sentence is enclosed within the parentheses. Place the period outside the parenthesis when the words enclosed in the parentheses are not a complete sentence.

> Put the cover on the engine. (Hand tighten the nuts.)
> Put the cover on the engine (with the arrow up).

(5) Place a period after some letters and numbers used in the standard English outline for reports. Do not place a period after numbers and letters that use a parenthesis. (See Chapter 7.)

> I.
>   A.
>   1.
>   a.
>   1)
>   a)

(6) Always place a period inside the quotation mark.

> "Turn off the switch."
> He was feeling rather "sick."

The Comma

(1) The comma is used for clarity to separate phrases, clauses, or terms that might otherwise be misunderstood.

> Mr. J. P. Evans, who was our vice-president, was elected president.
> Prior to the accident, several thunderstorms passed over the facility.

(2) The comma is used to separate words and numbers in a series.

The sound, light, heat, and chemical changes will be measured.
this comma can be eliminated

The numbers are: 47, 26, 33, 99, and 29.

(3) The comma is used to separate three or more adjectives that modify a noun.

We measured the intensity of the bright, pulsating, lightning bolts.

but:

We measured the pulsating lightning bolts.

(4) The comma is used to separate the city from a state. When inserted in a sentence, a comma also is used to separate the state from the rest of the sentence.

Brownsville, Texas
The facility will be built at Brownsville, Texas, where the mine is located.

(5) The comma is used to separate the day from the year in dates. When used in a sentence, the year is set off from the remainder of the sentence with a comma.

February 15, 1879 (conventional date style)

but:

February, 1999
On July 13, 1927, the mill first began operation.

(6) The comma is used to separate introductory clauses or phrases from the remainder of the sentence. Short phrases need not necessarily be set off with a comma.

introductory clause

Because he was tired, he moved the wrong switch.

introductory phrase

In a few minutes, the entire mill was shut down.

(7) The comma is used to separate an exact quote from the remainder of the sentence. The comma always is placed inside the quote.

"I first noticed sparks in the monitor set," he said.

(8) Use the comma between the last word of a series and the abbreviation "etc."

. . . heavy, dirty, etc.

Notice that no *and* is used between the last word of the series and *etc.* This is because *etc.* is the abbreviation of the Latin words *et cetera;* the word *et* means *and;* the word *cetera* means *so forth.*

(9) Use the comma to set off the name of a person being addressed from the rest of the sentence.

Mr. Dailey, I bid $2500 for that lumber.

(10) Use the comma to set off a person's name from his title whether it is used in a sentence or not. If the name and title are used in a sentence, a comma should also be used to separate the title from the remainder of the sentence.

Henry B. Louis, Jr.
John D. Davis, III
Bill Turner, Sheriff of Wash County
Herman J. Wong, Ph.D., and Dr. Simon H. Fry, M.D., were the co-directors of the project.

(11) Use a comma to set off a transitional word or expression from the remainder of the sentence (as, then, indeed, nevertheless, in addition, moreover, of course, therefore, etc.). If the transitional word is in the middle of the sentence, use commas on either side of the expression to separate it from the remainder of the sentence.

Of course, the lathe operator could not see the sparks. However, hot metal pieces were falling on workmen below.
The task seemed complete, however, and the job was closed.

(12) Use a comma to indicate the division of inverted names in directories, bibliographies, etc.

Jones, William H.
James, Harold H., M.D.

(13) Use a comma to set off numbers that are 10,000 and above. (See Chapter 4.)

9999 but: 99,999
1000 but: 10,000

(14) The comma is always placed inside of a quotation mark.

"Get ready to cut main power," the foreman said.

(15) Use a comma after the salutation in an informal letter and after the complimentary close in all letters.

	Formal	*Informal*
Salutation:	Gentlemen:	Dear Mr. Dawson,
Complimentary close:	Very truly yours,	Sincerely yours,

The Semicolon

(1) The semicolon is used to separate phrases containing commas. It is especially valuable in separating lists of names and titles, that contain commas, into meaningful groups.

> Guests were: John L. Space, LL.D., Ph.D.; Miss Adrian J. Smith, Ph.D., Director of Research; and George Syme, M.D.

(2) The semicolon is used to separate the two parts of a compound sentence . . . especially where a coordinating conjunction has been omitted.

> The chief engineer, who was in charge of the investigation, found defects in the soldering work; the remainder of the electrical work passed inspection.

(3) The semicolon is used to separate components in an internal paragraph listing:

> The foreman sent his men to get: (1) axes and crowbars; (2) picks and shovels; and (3) block and tackle.

External paragraph listing without the semicolon:

> The forman sent his men to get:
> (1) Axes and crowbars
> (2) Picks and shovels
> (3) Block and tackle

Notice that the first word in each external paragraph listing is always capitalized while the first word of an internal paragraph listing is not.

(4) Always place the semicolon outside quotation marks.
> "Start breaking into the room"; the foreman motioned with his hands.

(5) The semicolon is (almost without exception) placed outside the parentheses.

> The axes cut deep into the wood (they were very sharp); crowbars were used to pry the door open.

The Colon

(1) The colon is used to introduce an internal paragraph listing and an external paragraph listing.

> This annual stock sale will auction the following: (1) 350 cattle; (2) 233 hogs; and (3) 1000 sheep.
> This annual stock sale will auction the following:
>   (1) 350 cattle
>   (2) 233 hogs
>   (3) 1000 sheep

(2) The colon is used with a statement to introduce a direct quotation. Capitalize the first word after a colon if it expresses a complete thought or is a complete quote.

> After receiving the award, Harvey J. Jones, national champion, said: "I've waited all my life for this moment. It is a great honor for me to ..."

(3) The colon is used after a formal salutation in a letter.

> Dear Mr. Williams: Gentlemen:

(4) The colon is used to separate minutes from hours.

> 1:30 p.m. MST   1:30 p.m. EST

The Question Mark

The question mark is used to indicate a direct question. The question mark is placed inside quotation marks when it is part of the quoted material.

> "Is it now time to begin questioning?"
> The inspector said, "Is this a representative sample?"

The Exclamation Mark

The exclamation mark is used to indicate strong emotion. The exclamation mark is always placed inside the quotation.

> "He's there!"
> The foreman said, "Be careful!"

The Apostrophe

(1) The apostrophe is used to indicate the possessive form of a noun or a pronoun. If the noun or pronoun is singular,

add an ('s) to the word:

Jim's pulse was very weak.

However, if the noun is plural or ends in an "s," "x," "z," or "ce," add the (') after the last letter in the word:

This is Mr. Jones' house.
Fort Knox' Gold
Jazz' own trumpet
This is the Air Force' experimental plane.

(2) When showing the possessive form of abbreviations, such as GI, the following style is recommended.

Singular Nouns		*Plural Nouns*	
GI's	USAF's	Ph.D.s'	C.P.A.s'

(3) To form possessives from compound nouns or nouns in a series, add an ('s) for singular nouns not ending in "s" and (') after nouns ending in "s," "x," "ce," or "z."

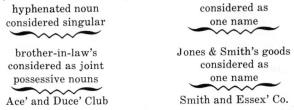

hyphenated noun considered singular	considered as one name
brother-in-law's	Jones & Smith's goods
considered as joint possessive nouns	considered as one name
Ace' and Duce' Club	Smith and Essex' Co.

(4) Use the apostrophe to indicate that letters have been left out of a word. This is an especially valuable tool in forming contractions (*don't* for do not; *it's* for it is; etc.). The practice of using the apostrophe to replace letters should be used with restraint, however.

Common Contractions

for will, shall, should, and would

I'll	we'll	you'll	he'll	they'll
I'd	we'd	you'd	he'd	they'd

For have and has

he's	they've	who's	it's

For am, is, and are

I'm	we're	you're	he's	it's	they're
who's	that's	there's	here's	where's	what's

For not

haven't	hasn't	needn't	can't	shan't
wouldn't	shouldn't	won't	don't	doesn't
isn't	aren't	wasn't	weren't	couldn't

Other Contractions

o'clock	for	of the clock
let's	for	let us
O'Sullivan	for	of Sullivan

(5) Do not use apostrophes with any abbreviations.

| Correct: | dept | Govt. | cont | |
| Incorrect: | dep't | Gov't. | cont'd | (These are common but inappropriate contractions.) |

(6) The apostrophe is often used for the omission of numbers when expressing general dates that indicate an era. However, this practice is not suitable when expressing actual dates.

Correct:	'49ers	the '30s
Correct:	June 16, 1849	the 1930s
Incorrect:	June 16, '49	

Parentheses

(1) Parentheses are used to separate ideas and thoughts from the main part of a sentence. They may be used in three different ways depending upon the meaning that the writer intends to give his words.

A phrase (or clause) within the sentence:

They carefully removed the damaged power unit (while smoke puffed from within).

A phrase (or clause) outside of a sentence:

They carefully removed the damaged power unit. (while smoke puffed from within)

Two sentences:

They carefully removed the damaged power unit. (Smoke puffed from within.)

Only if the material inside the parentheses is a complete sentence is there a period placed inside the parentheses. Words in parentheses (called parenthetical expressions) are always subordinate to the main sentence.

Do not use commas to separate parenthetical material from the associated sentence. The parentheses adequately separate the clause or phrase without commas.

(2) Parentheses are used in an internal or an external paragraph listing.

> This annual stock sale will auction the following: (1) 350 cattle; (2) 233 hogs; and (3) 1000 sheep.

or

> This annual stock sale will auction the following:
> (1) 350 cattle
> (2) 233 hogs
> (3) 1000 sheep

(3) Parentheses are used to enclose words of explanation.

> The table style (See Figure 4) is satisfactory.

or

> The table style is satisfactory. (See Fig. 4.)

(4) Parentheses are used to enclose numbers in legal documents and thereby avoid misunderstanding. However, this practice is not good style and is not recommended for use in regular vocational correspondence.

> He was awarded sixty dollars ($60.00). (legal form)
> He was awarded $60.00. (business form)

Quotation Marks

(1) Quotation marks are used to enclose a direct quotation.

> "I believe improper soldering was the cause," the foreman said.

(2) When consecutive paragraphs are quoted, the following style is recommended. Place a quote before each paragraph but only after the last paragraph.

> "According to information derived from a literature search, it was revealed that proof of a change in velocity of the AAA race car . . .
> "Here, a light ray passing through . . .
> "It is the purpose of this experiment to . . .
> "All drag races were performed using the NASCAR rules. Two vehicles were . . . and satisfactory."

(3) Place the following titles in quotes when using them in written matter.

Newspaper	"The New York Times"
Newspaper article	"Thief Takes Kitchen Sink"
Magazine	"Newsweek"
Magazine article	"Health Care for the Aged"
Book chapter	Chapter II, "Do or Die"
Brochure	"Aero Company's New Products"

Musical composition   "Saint Louis Blues"
Work of art   "Madonna and Child"
Report section   Section IV, "High Test Steel"

Book titles, report titles, paper titles, and titles of significant documents are underscored. Never quote a title and *also* underscore it. Never underscore the spaces between a series of words in a sentence.

Correct: You Can't Go Home Again (book title)
           Bill of Rights (significant document)
Incorrect: "You Can't Go Home Again"
           "You Can't Go Home Again"
           You Can't Go Home Again

The Hyphen

(1) The hyphen is used to join separate words together and thereby give additional meaning and clarity.

Joining adjectives that modify nouns:

       adjective

The small-scale fan motor was not functioning properly.

         adjective

The Journal presents up-to-the-minute news.

The hyphen is never used to join adverbs ending in *ly* to adjectives.

Correct: badly cut hand   newly elected officer
Incorrect: badly-cut hand   newly-elected officer

Joining words to make a noun:

        noun

A man, who said he was a passer-by, said he saw sparks emanating from the vent hole.

     noun

The Allen-Jones Steel Company will produce structural shapes.

(2) The hyphen is used to indicate a double occupation or office.

Secretary-Treasurer   author-lecturer
Treasurer-Comptroller   mechanic-driver

However, it is not proper to hyphenate titles that denote a single office such as vice president, commander in chief, sergeant at arms, ambassador at large, chief of police, etc.

(3) The hyphen is used to divide words at the ends of lines.

> The passer-by, who testi-
> fied at the investigation.

Use the *Webster's New Collegiate Dictionary* to determine the correct places to divide a word. Divide words preferably by *syllables* where the dots separate the letters. Words may also be divided at the accent marks.

> Preferred: dispro-portion-ate   testi-moni-al
> Also correct: dis-pro-por-tion-ate   tes-ti-mo-ni-al

When there are no dots in the word, it may be divided by the accent marks.

> Correct: anx-ious   eight-een   eve-ning
> hin-drance   morn-ing   sci-ence

It is proper to hyphenate any word between doubled consonants at the end of a line. For example:

> col-lation   cor-rect   mes-sage
> neces-sary   recom-mend   war-rant

It is not acceptable to hyphenate the last letter of a word. Hyphenating two letters of a word is acceptable. Do not hyphenate a proper name, Arabic numbers, abbreviations or contractions.

> Incorrect: San Fran-   George Wash-
> cisco   ington

Do not place the hyphen on the following line.

> Incorrect: ... the confirm   ... the end
> -ation   -ing

Divide hyphenated words only where the hyphen is located.

> Correct: high-
> spirited
> Incorrect: high-spirit-
> ed

Do not hyphenate the last word in a paragraph or the last word on a page. Rewriting should be able to shorten the paragraph to fit. Avoid dividing words at the end of two or more consecutive lines.

Do not hyphenate any one-syllable words such as:

| ask | asked | come | name | named | some | town |

(4) The hyphen is not used to separate prefix words from the suffix unless:

(a) The resulting word would be confusing

(b) The suffix is a proper noun

(c) The prefix ends in the same letter that begins the suffix

Avoid doubling letters between a prefix and a suffix by using a hyphen to separate them.

Common prefixes are:

anti	co	dis	ex-	ill-	inter
non	out	over	per	pre	pro
re	self-	semi	sub	trans	un

Correct:

coauthor	reclaim
co-operate (preferred)	re-edit
co-operation	re-elect
nonyielding	semiusable
non-Japanese	semi-Egyptian
non-noun	semi-independent
predawn	subsystem
pre-eminence	sub-African
pre-Victorian	sub-boarder
proconsul	unavailable
pro-American	un-American
pro-operational	unnamed (exception to rule)

Either could be correct, but the use of the hyphen here avoids misleading the reader:

recollect	or	re-collect
recount	or	re-count
recover	or	re-cover
reform	or	re-form
resign	or	re-sign

The prefixes *ex-, ill-, self-,* and *well-* are always hyphenated.

Correct: We make short-term and long-term loans.

| ex-president | ill-defined | self-employed |
| ex-social-chairman | ill-mannered | well-spoken |

The suffixes *-by, -down, -elect, -in,* and *-up* are always hyphenated.

Correct:

passer-by	run-down	make-up	president-elect
stand-by	stand-in	runner-up	senator-elect

(5) All numbers 21 and above that are combinations of two words are always hyphenated.

Correct:	twenty	forty	ninety
	twenty-one	forty-one	ninety-one
	twenty-five	forty-six	ninety-nine

It should be noted that correct style in vocational writing is to spell out all numbers less than 10 and write all numbers 10 and above in the Arabic form. (See Chapter 4.)

(6) All colors that are combinations of two words are hyphenated. For example:

blue-green   red-orange   yellow-gold   yellow-orange

(7) Do not suspend hyphenated words in a series.

Correct:	We make short-term and long-term loans.
	It was a two-year or a four-year contract.
Incorrect:	We make short- and long-term loans.
	It was a two- or a four-year contract.

(8) All words combined with the suffix *like* are written as solid words unless the prefix word ends in l.

Correct:	businesslike	but:	girl-like
	lifelike		flower like

(9) Words combined with *one* may be written as one word or two, or separately depending on the implied meaning.

Correct:	Any one	anyone
	every one	everyone
	no one	(always written as two words)
	some one	someone
For example:	Anyone may go.	
	Any one person may go.	

(10) Many multiple-word terms (particularly those joined by *of* and *to*) are hyphenated by usage when they are considered in context as one expression. For example:

bread-and-butter	give-and-take
bric-a-brac	grant-in-aid
(always hyphenated)	
change-of-address	
catch-as-catch-can	hit-or-miss
coast-to-coast	hit-and-run

hand-to-mouth

<table>
<tr><td>dyed-in-the-wool</td><td>horse-and-buggy</td></tr>
<tr><td>free-and-easy</td><td>man-of-war</td></tr>
<tr><td></td><td>(always hyphenated)</td></tr>
<tr><td>free-for-all</td><td>matter-of-course</td></tr>
<tr><td>mother-of-pearl</td><td></td></tr>
<tr><td>(always hyphenated)</td><td>run-of-the-mill</td></tr>
<tr><td>ne'er-do-well</td><td></td></tr>
<tr><td>(always hyphenated)</td><td>so-and-so</td></tr>
<tr><td>out-of-the-way</td><td>straight-from-the-shoulder</td></tr>
<tr><td>out-of-town</td><td>such-and-such</td></tr>
<tr><td>ready-to-wear</td><td>3-to-6 odds</td></tr>
<tr><td>right-of-way</td><td>up-to-date</td></tr>
<tr><td>rule-of-thumb</td><td>up-to-the-minute</td></tr>
</table>

(11) All *in-law* terms are hyphenated.

Correct:

brother-in-law	sister-in-law
daughter-in-law	son-in-law
mother-in-law	father-in-law

(12) A few multiple-word terms are now written as solid words:

counterclockwise	nonetheless
inasmuch	nowadays
nevertheless	theretofore

(13) When capital letters are used in connection with other terms, they are always hyphenated. For example:

A-bomb	A-frame	H-bomb	I-beam	S-curve
T-bone	T-square	U-turn	X-ray	V-necked

Consult your dictionary when in doubt as to whether a term is normally hyphenated or not. Always use the style prescribed by the dictionary when one is presented. When confronted with modifying compound adjectives and most other hyphenation problems, you will have to make your own decision about the term—based on rules previously discussed in this book.

The Dash

The dash is used to indicate an abrupt change in thought.

"Jim took no money—paper or coin—as he came out of the office," the witness said.

Your price of $10.00 per unit is satisfactory—if the shipping dates are met.

No spaces are placed on either side of a dash. When typing, remember that a dash is shown as two consecutive hyphens.

The Ellipsis

The ellipsis is used in a sentence to indicate that a word or words have been left out. When words are left out of a sentence, three dots are used:

The purpose of this test was to evaluate the installation procedure for conduit pipe . . . particularly near the boiler room.

Do not put spaces on either side of a sentence ellipsis. Never use more than three dots. When a paragraph (s) has been left out, three stars are used between those paragraphs remaining:

In the rigid electrical conduit pipe system, all wires are enclosed in a continuous galvanized iron or aluminum pipe which is smooth inside so that wires will not be damaged when they are drawn into it.

* * *

The conduit pipe is softer than ordinary galvanized water pipe for ease in making bends. The conduit is installed during building construction and . . .

APPENDIX C

Capitalization

There are firm rules and practices in the English language when it comes to the capitalization of words. Mainly, capitalization is used to place emphasis as indicated in the following examples. However, personnel in many companies tend to capitalize words needlessly. It is important *not* to capitalize needlessly because this practice is time consuming, and it is difficult to maintain a consistent writing style unless you adhere to normal writing practices.

The rules and practices of capitalization are:

(1) Capitalize the first word in every sentence.

> The first memorandum is incomplete.

(2) Capitalize all nouns that are the names of persons, places, or organizations.

> The case was manufactured by Smithson & Sons.
> The AFL-CIO is a large, labor-serving organization.

(3) Do not capitalize small words, such as and, of, the, for, from, with, etc., that appear in names of companies, names of organizations, and other titles unless they are the first word of the title, or unless the specific organization prefers the word to be capitalized.

> Money was sent by The Xavier and Scholar Company.

Notice that "The" is capitalized because it is part of the company's name.

(4) When the names of persons contain particles or fragments, such as da, d', della, von, van, etc., it is best to consult the preferred spelling of the individual person or company. It could be either:

> John d'Vacenta or John D'Vacenta

(5) Capitalize all titles of rank, honor, or respect when they are used with a proper noun.

> The Honorable Joseph I. Ebler will conduct the investigation.
> Now, Uncle John will conduct the investigation.
> John Allen, Business Manager, Plumbers & Steam Fitters Union Local No. 19, is coming next week.
> John Allen, Union General Chairman, will be there.
> They sent for the Reverend William H. Brown.
> It was Sheriff Turner who investigated the incident.

(6) Do not capitalize common titles when they are used alone.

> The carpenter came into the room.
> Jim's uncle came to the office when he heard of the incident.
> The foreman was angry.

(7) Do not capitalize common occupational titles or false titles no matter how they are used.

> Jim L. Smith, an accountant for our firm, was arrested.
> It is time for electricians Smith and Jones to begin stringing wire.

(8) Capitalize all titles of very important persons, even though the person's name is not used.

> the President (of a nation)
> the Pope (leader of a religious movement)
> the King (of a nation)
> the Vice President (of a nation)
> the Speaker of the House (of Representatives)

(9) Capitalize any word that is used in place of the name of a group or person in the Federal Government.

> the Nation (when referring to the United States)
> a Government official (when referring to the United States)
> in the Cabinet (when referring to the President's cabinet)
> the Senator (an elected Federal official)
> the Congressman (an elected Federal official)

(10) Capitalize the general name of any organization or group if the complete name has already been spelled out in an earlier part of your discussion.

> The Commission of American Labor will make the decision.
> This Commission is granted power by . . .

(11) In text, capitalize principal words in the specific name of any book, paper, report, or other document.

> the *Constitution of the United States* and: the Constitution
> *City Ordinance No. 10* (name of a document) but: the ordinance
> the *Bill of Rights* (name of a document) but: this document and this Bill
> *The Sloping Drain Field* (name of a report) but: the report

White Paper No. 13, Pollution Control (name of a paper) but: the paper
Form No. 22 (a document), but: the form

(12) In headings, capitalize the document title, major section headings and first level sideheadings. Subordinate sideheadings should begin with an initial capital.

FLOW OF PARTICLES

I. *Introduction*

  A. *Vat treatment process*
    1. *Heat factors*
      a. *Structural build-up*

(13) Capitalize all textual references to part of a specific document.

Chapter I	Introduction	List of Figures
Appendix	Index	Table of Contents
Foreword	Figure 14	Table II

(14) Capitalize a noun when it has the value of a proper noun.

The Vocational College is in California.
There are many unions and associations in this city.
The Union met at the Hall this week.
We believe in the Constitution.

(15) Capitalize principal words in the names of squares, parks, towers, monuments, statues, buildings, thoroughfares, bridges, tunnels, bodies of water, rivers, and mountains. In other words, capitalize the principal words in all recognized landmarks.

Liberty Park (a city park)
Empire State Building (a famous building)
the Capitol (when referring to a specific state or national building)
Ocean Park Drive (a thoroughfare)
Fifth Avenue (a thoroughfare)
The Washington Monument
The Lincoln Memorial (a building and a monument)
The Bay City Tunnel
the Golden Gate Bridge
Lake Champlain
the Great Salt Lake
Provo River
Gulf of Mexico
Persian Gulf
Mississippi River
Indian Ocean

Rocky Mountains
Mount Timpanogos

(16) When referring to buildings, departments, groups, sections, etc., within your company, the accepted practice is to capitalize them.

the Nondestructive Test Building
the Administration Building
the Drafting Department
the Design Group
the Photographic Section

(17) Do not capitalize seasons unless a date reference is specific.

in the spring of the year, but: the Spring of 1927

(18) Capitalize the days of the week and the months of the year.

Monday, Tuesday   June, July

(19) Capitalize all principal words in the titles of plays, musical compositions, art creations, and document titles.

Dial M for Murder (a play)
"The Madonna and Child" (a painting)
"Slaughter on Tenth Avenue" (a musical composition)
"Man on Horseback" (a sculpture)

(20) Capitalize only those abbreviations that represent a word that is normally capitalized or unless the abbreviation has been capitalized by custom.

number   No.   American Rocket Society   ARS
Fahrenheit F   International Office Machines, Inc.   IOM

(21) Capitalize all trade names in the manner established by the company that sells the product or service.

Ivory soap   VapoRub   DupliMAT   Mel-Cal finish

Notice that some trade names have unusual capitalization and spelling.

(22) Capitalize only the second term in a hyphenated word if the second term is normally capitalized and the first term is not.

inter-American   non-Russian

However, if the entire hyphened word is used in a title or is the first word in a sentence, the word should be capitalized.

Inter-American Council   Non-Russian Committee

(23) Capitalize the first word in a complete quotation when it is used in another sentence.

>Mr. Smith said, "It's not true."

(24) If you are in doubt as to whether a commonly used word needs to be capitalized or not, look it up in the dictionary.

>It's:
>
>| | |
>|---|---|
>| X-ray not x-ray | centigrade not Centigrade |
>| Fahrenheit not fahrenheit | Kelvin not kelvin |

(25) Capitalize principal words in the names of holidays, historical events, historical periods, religious days, etc.

>| | | |
>|---|---|---|
>| Mother's Day | Halloween | Feast of the Passover |
>| Labor Day | World War II | the Renaissance |

(26) Descriptive terms for regions and locations should be capitalized.

>| | |
>|---|---|
>| the Deep South | the Far West |
>| the Orient | the Empire State |
>| the Intermountain Area | out West |

(27) Do not capitalize points of the compass unless they are used in connection with a geographical location.

>| | |
>|---|---|
>| north | Northern States |
>| south-southeast | the Southwest |

(28) The sun, moon, earth, and stars are not capitalized unless they are listed in reference to other celestial bodies.

>The sun is hot.
>
>The earth is two billion years old.
>
>but:
>
>The first leg of the journey will be from the Earth to Venus.
>
>The North Star is much larger than our Sun.

(29) Principal words in the name of any official government or judicial body are capitalized.

>United States Supreme Court
>
>The California Court of Appeals
>
>The Utah State Legislature
>
>The United States Senate
>
>the City Commission

(30) Many words that were once capitalized are no longer capitalized because they have acquired an independent meaning that is no longer associated with the original source of the word.

>| | |
>|---|---|
>| portland cement | macadamized roads |
>| roman style type | plaster of paris |
>| artesian water | |

(31) All words that denote Deity, names in the Bible, and other sacred words are capitalized.

God	Son	Buddha
He	Heaven	Nirvana
Him	Hades (but: hell)	Zeus
Father	Satan	Venus

(32) The names of recognized events are capitalized.

The Rose Bowl	but: the bowl
The Kentucky Derby	but: the derby
the World Series	but: the series

(33) Do not capitalize common nouns when they are not used as part of the official name.

Lake Ontario	but: the lake
Glen Canyon Dam	but: the dam
Scouts of America	but: the scouts

(34) Principal words in military decorations are capitalized.

Bronze Star
Congressional Medal of Honor
Distinguished Flying Cross

Glossary of Vocational Writing Terms

A

Abbreviations—letters or groups of letters which represent or are a substitute for words. They are valuable in effective writing because they save time and space. Only standard, well-known abbreviations should be used in most vocational writing situations.

Abstracts—a library reference system, wherein current periodical articles on technical subjects are summarized; a summary of a written report or document, including conclusions and recommendations.

Acknowledgments—a page in a document which gives credit to sources (people, documents, organizations, etc) from which material was gathered.

Ampersand—a symbol & used in company names (only) to replace the word *and*.

Appendix—a supplement section attached to the main body of a report or other documents. Information and data are listed in an appendix to avoid overpowering the discussion with too much detail.

Arabic numbers—1, 2, 5, 10, 50, 100, etc. (See any standard collegiate dictionary.)

B

Back-up document—a document printed on both sides of each page. Odd numbered pages should always appear on the right-hand side of a document if it is printed on both sides of the paper.

Bibliography—a list of documents relative to a given subject. It: (1) directs the reader to sources of material used in a given report; (2) permits the author of a report to acknowledge sources of information; and (3) aids readers in finding additional information on the same subject.

Binding—methods used to attach the individual pages of a document together other than hard cover books. Common techniques are (1) stapling; (2) stapling and applying tape to the bound edge; (3) punching holes and using mechanical or ring binders; and (4) punching holes and inserting plastic or spiral binders.

C

Callout—a written label on a figure which has an arrow pointing to a specific item in the image area.

Cartesian coordinate system—a system of line graphing which shows numerical relationships. It is based on the concept that numbers may be displayed as equal segments on a straight line. The lines may be either horizontal X axis or vertical Y axis, or a combination of the two axes. Both negative and positive numbers may be plotted within the system; the total system contains four quadrants.

Classified information—data and facts which are critical to the security of a government. Three general classifications used in the United States are: confidential, secret and top secret.

Clause—a group of related words containing a subject and a verb. Two general types include the *independent* and *dependent* forms.

Clearness—writing with common words and phrases. Avoid the highfalutin words which may need to be defined.

Clichés—old, worn-out phrases which have no value in sentence construction.

Collation—to assemble, in correct sequence, the pages of a document.

Colloquialism—a word or expression which is common to a geographical region and not considered part of formal English. Most slang terms are colloquial.

Compass (pencil)—an illustration tool used to draw circles.

Conciseness—writing with an economy of words, yet with enough words to tell the full story.

Conclusion—a final part of a report which states the results of evaluating data and/or facts presented in the text of that report.

Concreteness—use of words in writing which have specific meaning. For example, *large* could be 3 in. or 3 mi.

Consistency—Writing which uses the same words for the same object or situation each time. This practice aids the reader in understanding what the writer means to say.

Copy—the written part of a document.

Creativity—five mental stages used by man to improve a situation or solve a problem. The stages include: preparation, incubation, illumination, evaluation, and reconstruction.

D

Description—writing which mentally paints a picture of an object or a situation in the reader's mind. Words which identify size, shape, color, distance, material of construction, texture, finish, condition, hardness, etc., are employed to enhance the reader's understanding.

Directness—writing which wastes no words and comes directly to the point.

Direct object—names the receiver of transitive verb action in a sentence. Example: She hit *him*.

Discussion—the middle part of a report which tells what the alternate possibilities are for solving the problem stated in the introduction, and which also states the results of testing the proposed solutions.

Distribution—methods of transmitting documents to the proper recipients.

Distribution list—a list of people, offices, or organizations that will receive copies of a particular document.

Document—any formal, written publication.

Draft—a specific stage of development in writing a document in which a whole entity has been completed. The sequence usually follows this pattern: rough draft (perhaps hand-written); typed rough draft; second typed draft . . . and final manuscript.

Drawing—an image of a physical object or location shown by a combination of line, symbolic shading, or solid mass, or any one or more of these. In printing a drawing is photographed as line and mass, but not as half-tone screen.

E

Editing—to remove, add, correct, and rearrange elements of a written communication. The object of editing is to improve the quality of the communication.

Effective communications—when the reader understands what the writer has written, and the writer has told all necessary facts.

Exaggeration—writing which enlarges the real circumstances beyond the realm of truth.

Exponent—a number expressed as a power of ten. For example, this number 2,330,000 expressed in powers of ten equals 2.33×10^6; and a decimal may be written with a negative exponent, 0.000014 equals 1.4×10^{-5}.

F

Facts—the basic information and data used to construct a document.

Figurative language—writing characterized by vague comparisons between reality and imaginative relationships. Figures of speech.

Figure—a general term for any drawing, photograph, or graph which appears in a document.

Flow diagram—a special type of drawing which shows a progressive sequence of events. Words enclosed in a rectangle describe an individual event, and an arrow projecting from that rectangle to the next rectangle shows the direction of the flow of events.

Footnote—a note at the bottom of a page which gives supplementary information about the topic under discussion.

Foreword—a page in a technical document which states the purpose for publication of that document.

Format—the physical dimensions of a document, including: page size, figure and table sizes, text size. The outline style of major headings and sideheadings.

French curve—an illustration tool used to draw smooth curves on a drawing.

G

Gerund—a verb form used in a sentence as a noun. It must have an *ing* ending. Example: *Driving* an automobile requires training. (*Driving* is used as noun subject of sentence.)

Grammar—the study of all those rules that treat the construction, form, and usage of words.

Graphs—drawings that show mathematical relationships. Types include the bar graph, the circle graph, and the line graph.

Grid—a network of uniformly spaced horizontal and vertical lines for locating points by means of a coordinate approach.

H

Heterogeneous—consisting of things that are not alike, or not of the same class.

Histogram—a bar graph in which bars of various lengths are used on a scaled ratio to indicate mathematical values.

Homogeneous—consisting of things that are alike.

I

Image—the item being portrayed in a figure.

Image size—the common size of a figure or of text on a document page. (6¼″ × 8½″ on a 8½″ × 11″ sheet is recommended size for full-page figures.)

Indexes—card catalog sections and other reference setups in a library where technical information may be obtained.

Infinitive—a verb form used in a sentence as a noun, adjective, or an adverb. An infinitive consists of the root verb preceded by the word "to." Example: *To run* is fun. (noun subject of sentence).

Input—source data from which a document is prepared.

Instruction—a series of statements which tell a reader how to accomplish a goal.

Interviewing—the technique of obtaining information for use in document preparation by asking questions of witnesses or authorities. Questions may be written or oral.

Introduction—the beginning part of a report which states the purpose of the study discussed in the report and gives necessary background information. The introduction states the problem under consideration.

L

Line weight—the thickness of a line in a drawing or on a table.

List of figures—a page in a document which lists figures found in that document and the page where each figure may be viewed.

List of tables—a page in a document which lists tables found in that document and the page where each table may be found.

Logic—reasoning (thinking) that has no fault with respect to reality, or to a particular frame of reference.

M

Mean—the sum of all numerical values divided by the total number of values.

Median—the mid-value of data, where half of the numerical values are the same as or greater than the mid-value and half the numerical values are the same as or less than the mid-value.

Mode—the value in numerical data which occurs most often.

N

Notes—the written statements and data used to prepare a report or other document.

O

Objectivity—writing which does not make unrealistic statements or conclusions.

Observation—a specific examination of a measuring device or situation at a particular point in time. Numerical or worded data from the observation is recorded for use in document preparation.

Offset printing—a reproduction method with these steps: (1) metal, plastic or paper plates are placed on a printing press; (2) the press (operated by electric power) deposits ink on the image area of the plate; (3) the inked image is then taken from the plate and deposited on a blanket; and (4) the image is transferred from the blanket to the printing paper.

Outline—a plan for writing a document. The main type used by vocational writers is the heading outline, where headings are noted in brief phrases or single words and are numbered or lettered consistently according to their rank in the report. General types include the standard English outline, the numerical outline, and the position and weight outline.

Outline, scientific—a report outline that is based on the scientific method of reasoning. The outline includes these components: (1) introduction (states the problem); (2) discussion (proposes solution and gives results of testing the solution); and (3) conclusions and recommendations.

P

Paragraph—one or more sentences which represent like thoughts about a related topic. A paragraph is an intermediate part of any written composition—usually larger than a single sentence, yet usually smaller than the entire composition. Paragraph forms include: unresolved paragraph, inductive paragraph, deductive paragraph, and inductive-deductive paragraph.

Participle—a verb form used in a sentence as an adjective. Example: They examined the *shattered* structure. (*Shattered* modifies *structure*.)

Phrase—a group of two or more related words not containing a subject and a verb. A phrase serves in the sentence as a single part of speech.

Predicate—those words which talk about a subject in a sentence, including the verb, object, complement, and any modifiers of these elements.

Preface—a page near the front of a document which presents useful information about that document.

Prefatory elements—those items which appear in a document before the text (or body), including: transmittal letter, abstract (or summary), title page, foreword, contents page, list of figures page, list of tables page, etc.

Pride of authorship—a psychological condition in which we cannot or will not see the faults in our own writing.

Proofreading—reading a written communication to determine the correctness of all elements. When errors are found, the proofreader indicates these mistakes by use of specific symbols. Typists correct the errors.

Proprietary information—facts which should not be discussed with people outside a given company or group.

Protractor—an illustration tool used to draw precise angles.

Punctuation—13 marks and symbols that are used in sentence construction to make the words more meaningful.

Q

Questionnaire—a form submitted to a sampling or specific group of people which asks questions about a topic. Data gathered in this manner is often included in reports and other technical documents.

R

Range—the difference between upper and lower limits of numerical data.

Recommendation—a final part of a report which suggests future plans that are based on evaluation of test data and/or facts presented in the text of that report.

Reproduction—any method used to make copies of a document. Common methods include: Xerox, offset press, mimeograph, and spirit duplicator.

Restraint—writing which does not distort the real situation (under discussion) beyond reasonable truth. Writing with no exaggerations.

Roman numerals—I, II, V, X, L, C, etc. (See any standard collegiate dictionary.)

S

Sampling—the principle of testing a representative fraction of a group. This fraction is assumed to be a statistically valid quantity that substitutes for testing the whole group.

Scientific method—a process of reasoning in which problems are solved. The method has six steps: (1) problem exists, (2) obtain facts about problem, (3) study facts, (4) propose solution, (5) test solution, and (6) formulate conclusion.

Section—A major part of a report or other document.

Sentence—a self-contained speech unit, containing a subject and a verb, which expresses a complete thought. Sentences are classified by function, structure, and style.

Specifications—a series of statements which tell a reader what the expected results of an activity should be.

Speech, parts of—the eight basic word forms from which sentences are formed, including: nouns, pronouns, verbs, adjectives, adverbs, prepositions, conjunctions, and interjections.

Standard deviation—the square root of the *variance* in numerical data. (See **variance.**)

Style—a manner of writing, which, if satisfactory, facilitates rapid reading, conveys the exact meaning, shows restraint, is objective, and is clear for future reference.

Subject—that word or group of words in a sentence which is being talked about by the remainder of the words in the sentence.

Subjective complement—describes or renames the subject of a sentence. If the complement is a noun, it renames the subject: He is *president*. If the complement is an adjective, it describes the subject: She is *pretty*.

Subsection—a minor part of a report or other document; a part of a section.

Summary—a condensed version of pertinent information contained in a document. A summary should also include conclusions and recommendations.

Supplementary elements—those items which may appear in a report after the main body, including: appendixes, bibliography, acknowledgments, index, list of abbreviations, glossary, etc.

Syllogism—a formal argument, consisting of a major premise, a minor premise, and a conclusion.

> All copper wire will conduct electric current.
> This rod is copper wire.
> _____
> ∴ (Therefore) this rod will conduct electric current.

Symbols, proofreading—special symbols used in proofreading technique to indicate changes and corrections.

Symmetrical—an object, sentence, drawing, etc., which has two equal parts; balanced proportions.

Symmetry—writing with balanced and equal parts. (For example, a compound sentence with approximately the same number of words in each independent clause.)

Syntax—a logical and orderly arrangement of words, phrases, clauses, sentences, and paragraphs.

T

Table—a presentation of word and/or numerical data in which one set of facts will be compared in columns against another set of facts.

Table of contents—a page in a document which lists the major sections and subsections and tells the page numbers where these sections may be found.

Teutonic language—a Germanically related language.

Text—the paragraphing part of a document. The body of a document.

Textual elements—those items which make up the body of a report, including: introduction, discussion, and conclusions and recommendations.

Thoroughness—writing which tells enough, but not too much.

Thumbnail sketch—a rough outline.

Title—the name of a document, table, figure, section, or other major element of a report.

Title page—the first page of a report or other document which tells the reader: document title, publication date, period covered by document, name of writer(s), name of person(s) giving approval, or other general information.

Transitions—words such as *thus, but, however, furthermore,* etc., which are used in writing to more smoothly blend sentences and paragraphs together. Normally, these words begin a sentence or paragraph.

Transmittal letter—a brief business letter which tells the reader what he has received—a document, materials, etc.

Triangle—an illustration tool used to make specific angle lines on a drawing: 90°, 60°, 30°, etc.

Typographical error—an error in typing, not necessarily spelling.

V

Vagueness—writing which does not make the meaning clear, either because obscure words are used, or because complicated sentences and paragraphs are constructed, or because sentences or paragraphs do not have a proper sequence.

Variance—the sum of the squares of the differences between individual numerical values and the mean value, all divided by the total number of values:

$$\frac{(a - b)^2 + (c - b)^2 \ldots + (z - b)^2}{n}$$

Where: a, c, z = individual values or numbers

b = the mean value

n = total number of values, including only one b.

Verb—a part of speech in a sentence that expresses action, existence or occurrence—relative to a subject.

Verbal—a verb form used in a sentence as another part of speech. Types include: *gerunds* used as nouns, *participles* used as adjectives, and *infinitives* used as nouns, adjectives or adverbs.

Index

All Italicized words or phrases refer to defined terms within a section on Correct Word Usage. Bold faced numbers refer to page numbers of illustrations.